THE
CONFIDENT
HOUSE HUNTER

**a home inspector's tips for
finding *your* perfect house**

THE
CONFIDENT
HOUSE HUNTER

a home inspector's tips for
finding *your* perfect house

DYLAN CHALK

Plain Sight Publishing
An Imprint of Cedar Fort, Inc.
Springville, Utah

ISBN 13: 978-1-4621-1897-7

Published by Plain Sight Publishing, an imprint of Cedar Fort, Inc.
2373 W. 700 S., Springville, UT 84663
Distributed by Cedar Fort, Inc., www.cedarfort.com

LIBRARY OF CONGRESS CATALOGING-IN-PUBLICATION DATA

    Names: Chalk, Dylan, 1970- author.
    Title: The confident house hunter : a home inspector's tips and tricks for
      finding your perfect house / Dylan Chalk.
    Description: Springville, Utah : Plain Sight Publishing, an imprint of Cedar
      Fort, Inc., [2016] | Includes bibliographical references and index.
    Identifiers: LCCN 2016003909 (print) | LCCN 2016005341 (ebook) | ISBN
      9781462118977 (perfect bound : alk. paper) | ISBN 9781462126781 (epub,
      pdf, mobi)
    Subjects: LCSH: House buying. | Building inspection.
    Classification: LCC HD1379 .C47 2016 (print) | LCC HD1379 (ebook) | DDC
      643/.12--dc23
    LC record available at http://lccn.loc.gov/2016003909

Cover design by Krystal Wares and Kinsey Beckett
Cover design © 2016 by Cedar Fort, Inc.
Edited and typeset by Rebecca Bird

Printed in the United States of America

10 9 8 7 6 5 4 3 2 1

Printed on acid-free paper

To Mom and Dad

CONTENTS

CONTENTS

ACKNOWLEDGMENTS

I t feels a little unjust to mark a single person's name as the author of a book. In my limited experience, a book does not emanate from a solitary person; a book is a collage of observations born of experiences and relationships, and the author is simply the lunatic ringleader who is in charge of getting it all down. As I am lucky enough to call myself the ringleader for this particular project, I feel in great debt to many people who have contributed wittingly or otherwise to my life and to this book.

Mom and Dad for everything: Mom for her loving criticism, editing, and encouragement; and Dad, I miss you terribly and wish you could read this book. My sweet wife, Margot, and my superlative boys—you are my pride and joy! Peter, Molly, Marian, Matt, Henry, Miles, and Graham for being my loving extended family. Kevin Hawkins—PR guru, writing mentor, and successful prodder of this project. Raj Hayden—my mentor and friend, without whose help this book would not exist. To all the folks at Cedar Fort, Inc., and especially to Chelsea Jackson for believing in and advocating for this book. Tory and the gang at All Media Bainbridge. All my Seattle friends, colleagues, teachers, and mentors; notably Kahlia Root, Nick O'Connell, and Dave Smith. Girl Friday Productions and especially Andrea Dunlop for your keen wisdom and insights. Randy Near and Jed Ballou—my partners and friends who have encouraged and facilitated this dream. Nancy at Enlightened Edits. Christin Camacho, Chad Dierickx, and other folks at Redfin who have been supportive of my writing about home inspection. Chuck Ramey for his wisdom, feedback, and encouragement. Geord, Benj, and Dave: my lifelong crew. The CC gang . . . you know who you are. My older buddies, heroes, and mentors:

ACKNOWLEDGMENTS

Leland, Will, and Smash for the inspiring way you all charge into life. Jill Kneerim for being kind and generous with your valuable time. Michael and Dudley for your nudge toward the everlasting gift of education and for supporting me during a very difficult time; I can't thank you enough. Most important, to all of my clients for whom I have done home inspections and to all the real estate professionals, friends, family, and acquaintances who have referred and trusted my home inspection business. Thank you!

INTRODUCTION

Finding the house that is right for *you* is harder than ever. In hot city markets, inventory is tight, competition is fierce, and inspection contingency periods are dwindling. In slower markets, stagnant and depressed house prices have resulted in deferred maintenance and murky transactions for bank-owned properties and foreclosures. Throughout the country, homes are requiring a larger percentage of our net worth to buy and sell. We are collectively taking greater risks with more expensive and more complex houses. Add to this housing bubbles, detailed home inspection reports, sewer inspections, marketing with edited images, crafty staging, Byzantine financing requirements, and a generally aging housing stock. It has never been more important for a homebuyer to develop skills for looking at and understanding houses.

Though you might think otherwise, it's likely that you are unprepared to look at houses. Like most people, you have probably learned to look at homes based on the "bling"—the big views, shiny kitchen countertops, rich hardwood floors, open floor plans, and sunken soaking tubs. That's not surprising. We are living in a gilded age of house consumerism and these are the things that are sold to us daily. Real estate sells the sizzle, not the steak.

As a prospective homebuyer, you probably spend more time looking at this sizzle than any generation of homebuyers before you. You are one of the 100 million visitors who flock each month to the top three real estate websites alone. Mix in reality TV shows, video channels dedicated solely to homes, millions of weekend open houses, tens of millions of online virtual tours, tens of thousands of local full-color sales magazines, and a million classified advertisements offering homes for sale. As a nation we seem to be obsessed with the prospect of a new house.

This obsession makes sense. The home is the cornerstone of the American dream. It is a concrete expression of our lifestyle, our freedom, our individualism, and our success. One's home remains the single greatest purchase *and* the single greatest investment for the vast majority of American families. Even with housing bubbles, the purchase of a home remains the single best money-saving mechanism available to Americans. Yet for many of us, the enormous purchase of a home is based on emotion and appearance rather than substance and knowledge.

THE OLD WAY TO SHOP FOR A HOME DOESN'T WORK

Did anyone ever teach you how to really "look" at a house? Nobody ever taught me. It was not until I started my professional home inspection training that I began to really look at houses and, even then, the training was focused on a system-by-system approach, which is the foundation of any good home inspection training but is inadequate as a stand-alone approach to seeing and understanding houses.

The art to looking at houses is to be able to zoom in close and scrutinize detail, and then pull back to take in the larger context of the house and even the neighborhood. The training I had was fantastic in a technical close-up sense, but it lacked this pulled-back panoramic point of view. This book weaves these two together so you can learn to use a manageable amount of the smaller details to help you see the larger picture and the larger picture to help you predict the small details.

The old model of real estate shopping assumes that you don't need to know how to do this because this is what your Realtor, your appraiser, and your home inspector will do for you. Unfortunately, this is a broken model. Why? Because it's *your* home, not theirs.

Keep this guiding principle in mind: It is exceedingly rare to find a house that nobody should buy at any price, yet at the same time, there are no perfect houses. **Every house is a great house for the right person at the price.** Understanding this, you can realize that the trick to finding *your* perfect house is to have your expectations aligned with the house.

Your real estate broker and your home inspector can facilitate discovery and provide guidance and advice, but they cannot make this happen. *This is something you do for yourself.* You will have to live with your home purchase decision for the next 5 to 30 years—or more—and selling your house could cost you 10 percent of its value after real estate fees and taxes. The time you invest now to learn how to see the "bones" and not just the "bling" could save you both emotional and financial turmoil and can make the process of looking for a home fun and rewarding rather than scary and intimidating.

This book helps you develop a structural awareness when looking at houses. You will learn to evaluate homes critically:

1. Learn about home systems in a unique way that helps prioritize their relative importance. Home systems are broken into three categories: **core**, **entrenched**, and **disposable**.
2. Discover innovative new ways to sort homes. Sort by age, owner, type, and architectural style.
3. Reduce the fear of the unknown and prepare yourself for the home-buying process by developing knowledge about critical home systems.
4. Build skills for comparing and contrasting different homes.
5. Develop vocabulary for describing houses and house systems.
6. Learn to see past a home's "staging" so you can start to see houses with the critical eye of a home inspector.
7. Gain the context to better understand why all houses have problems and where you might expect to find those problems.
8. Finally, learn techniques for evaluating risk so that your expectations are appropriate and your surprises diminished.

WHY DO I NEED TO LEARN TO LOOK AT HOUSES? WHAT'S THE DIFFERENCE BETWEEN HOUSES?

Most products we buy today are made in the context of highly regulated industries, but houses are an exception. Let's contrast houses with the other very expensive things we buy . . . cars. Autos are mass-produced by multibillion-dollar corporations. They are manufactured in a highly regulated industry, monitored by the federal government to adhere to stringent safety standards, and their performance is scrutinized by dozens of consumer advocacy groups.

New home building and the maintenance of existing homes are different. It's true that local county governments and city building officials regulate new construction, but existing homes have virtually no regulations at all. Houses don't have powerful advocacy groups calling for repairs and maintenance, and unlike cars, advances in the various systems and attributes of the modern home have gone largely unnoticed.

Yet, today's homes are more prone to problems as a result of our effort to make them more comfortable, convenient, and energy efficient. As homes get more expensive, so do their repairs and upkeep. And as homes age, their annual maintenance costs can quickly overwhelm the unprepared budget.

The reality is this: Homes are the most expensive purchases most of us will ever make. They are more complex than cars. They come in a virtually unlimited variety of shapes, sizes, and locations, yet most of us have never learned strategies or disciplines to "see" houses or think critically about them.

WHAT THIS BOOK WILL *NOT* DO

This book will not make you a home inspector and it is *not* a substitute for a quality home inspection. This book will not help you look at homes like a designer or a Realtor or an architect; those points of view are important and valid, but are not the focus here. This book will not drown you in technical terms. You will get the basic tools and technical knowledge you'll need to really see the bones of a home in simple, plain English.

This book is for you if

- You are a homebuyer or think you may become a homebuyer someday.
- You are a homeowner and you are interested in houses.
- You are helping someone buy a home (you are an agent, broker, appraiser, or home inspector).
- You love looking at houses.
- You just received a home inspection report and are freaking out.

WHAT THIS BOOK *WILL* DO

The Confident House Hunter will change the way you look at houses by giving you the tools and knowledge you need to see them with a trained eye. If you are a homebuyer, it will prepare you for the homebuying process by teaching you how to look critically at that which you aspire to buy, and educated homebuyers hold the following distinct advantages over those who are less prepared. Informed homebuyers:

- Know what they want and waste less time looking for it.
- Enjoy the process of house-hunting more because knowledge is fun and empowering while ignorance is scary and intimidating.
- Cope assertively with the fast-paced realities of short inventory and short inspection contingency periods.
- Manage detailed home inspection reports and disclosure with cogency and skill because they have the tools and point of view required for understanding context.
- Get surprised less because they go into homes with their eyes open.
- Waste less money on inspection fees.

The information presented in this book is not theoretical. I use the knowledge, skills, and strategies outlined here every day to help my clients better understand what they are proposing to buy. The genesis of this book is the acknowledgment that my clients would be so much better off if they had this information *before* they hired me—*before* the home inspection. That is why I wrote this book—to help homebuyers come to the home inspection prepared and informed. Now that you know what this book will do for you, let's begin the journey.

Best,

Dylan Chalk

Orca Inspection Services, LLC

PART I

The Philosophy

LEARNING TO SEE **1**

I t has always struck me that plastic surgeons must see people's faces differently than I do. After spending years studying the biology, structure, and features of the human face and learning how to manipulate those features, a person is bound to come away looking at faces differently. The same is true for houses.

This thought was brought home to me one day while I was training a new home inspector. My trainee, Randy, and I were driving across the I-90 bridge, heading west across Lake Washington into Seattle. It was a beautiful Pacific Northwest winter afternoon, purple light filtering through a smattering of clouds and sunlight winking off the icy peaks of the Olympic Mountains in the distance.

The I-90 bridge leads into a tunnel that was bored into a hillside on which a classic old Seattle neighborhood sits. It's typical Seattle—an array of houses ranging from 100 years old to brand new. Crossing the bridge, Randy commented on a lovely old house that looked to be built in the 1910s to 1920s. It had an elegant roofline, a gorgeous front porch, and a round turret with full southeastern exposure and a remarkable view of the fourteen-thousand-foot Mount Rainier.

"That's a beautiful house," he exclaimed.

I responded, "I bet the windows leak in the turret and the front porch is sagging down the hill."

Randy laughed. "You can't enjoy just looking at a house, can you?" he asked.

"I do enjoy looking at houses!" I insisted. My comments weren't intended to disparage that beautiful old house. Rather, I was simply

9

acknowledging the fact that as a home inspector, I have come to expect problems in even the most well cared for houses. All homes have design vulnerabilities; it is a home inspector's job to see them.

This is the point of view homebuyers need to have when looking at homes. Once you remove emotion from the equation, you can begin to really "see" a house and better understand potential problems from a logical and historical context. If problems are discovered during inspection, you have no need to be scared or surprised. Problems with houses tend to make sense, and, once you can recognize vulnerable areas for yourself, you'll see that they fit into a logical and somewhat expected pattern that is just another part of the house you are buying . . . or not buying.

The concept of the "trained eye" is at the heart of this book. But even so, two people with trained eyes will view things differently. Every person approaches life from his or her own point of view, and the bias created by personal experiences and preferences can never be fully culled from observation. There is no such thing as an unbiased point of view—we see what we want to see and what we are trained to see. When it comes to the largest investment you will ever make in your life, to be totally dependent on the points of view of other people—including the people you hire, like your Realtor or your home inspector—is to approach that investment from a point of weakness and vulnerability. That is why it is so important to develop skills for looking at houses.

In the rest of this chapter, I hope to use some of my experiences with clients and in life to illustrate why educating yourself in the game of home buying is so critical, and how you can gain the tools to make a skillful go of it. These stories will prepare you for the more technical chapters that are to follow.

HAVING THE RIGHT EXPECTATIONS: WHAT DO YOU REALLY WANT FROM A HOME?

Recently, I did a home inspection on a 60-year-old grandma house. I call it that because it is an actually category, meaning the home has been under the same ownership for quite a long time. I loved the house. It was in a great location. It had a simple underlying design that could, with a little work, be a classy, unique, low-maintenance, durable, and reliable home. It also had a nice yard and was well landscaped. It had an elegant mid-century modern flair. For decades its owner—an older woman—had lovingly maintained it. The house was a like a time capsule from the 1950s, with original kitchen appliances and Pepto-Bismol bathroom tile featuring matching toilets and sinks. I wanted to buy it myself.

The homebuyers—my clients, Pam and Don—came with me for the home inspection. Although they were there in body, they were mentally distracted—Don was following me while trying to keep his three-year-old son occupied, and Pam was swaddling a new baby girl, struggling to keep her asleep. Despite their divided attention, I did manage to learn from Don that this was at the top of their price range, and they were not going to have money to do much in the way of repairs. Plus, the Realtor had informed me that there was going to be heavy competition for this house and it might get bid up beyond their price range.

When I finished the inspection I looked at my clients. They looked exhausted; simply struggling through the home inspection had worn them out.

Now, I do not tell people what to do during a home inspection. It's not my place nor is it my job. My goal is to help my clients understand what they are buying so that they can make an informed decision. Most important, I want their expectations to be in alignment with what I see. Sometimes I find that storytelling is a more effective way of communicating this than just laying out technical mumbo jumbo. So I started sharing a bit of my own experience.

"You know, I bought a house that needed even more work than this and it was not nearly as nice a house as this," I began. "I had to fix just about everything in my house and I did it myself. It was a lot of labor, but it worked out really well for me in the end."

Don started to smile; Pam looked more cautious.

"The problem was, I had no life," I added. "My friends and my wife thought I had disappeared, because every free moment I had I was working on my house. It was as though I had vanished off the face of the earth for 2 years. And I was lucky. We didn't have kids yet, and I had the tools and the skills to be able to do much of the work myself. Without that, the project could have gotten very expensive. It probably would have gotten away from me. I can't even imagine trying to do all that with my kids now."

I could tell by the look on their faces that they were starting to see how much work they would be signing on for if they bought this house.

REALITY CHECK: UPDATED HOUSE VERSUS WELL CARED FOR HOUSE

There is a big difference between a house that has been well cared for and a house that has been updated. This nice little grandma house had not been updated since Dwight D. Eisenhower was president. The house had a great roofline, a nice new roof covering, a solid foundation, solid framing, great siding, easy access to systems, no drainage problems, and no deferred maintenance. In short, the house had great bones but many of the systems were old. The wiring and the plumbing may have worked all right for grandma, but they were not going to respond well to the rigors of family use. The house needed a laundry list of repairs, improvements, and updates: new supply pipes, a new waste pipe, a new boiler, a new water heater, a new electric panel, extensive wiring updates, new kitchen appliances, new laundry facilities, and some new flooring. A few of these updates were urgent.

Moreover, the house could have used a slew of other improvements: it had little to no attic insulation, the single pane windows were not operating well, and the bathrooms were going to be unreliable until updated.

And, on top of all this, there was one more big challenge. Some of the renovation work on this house would either need to be done prior to moving in, or it would necessitate moving the family elsewhere while work was under way due to the potential of lead and asbestos exposure during construction.

The reality of the situation was simple: great house, wrong client. Pam and Don were too busy with a new family and did not have the money or the time that this house would require to convert it from a well cared for grandma house to a reliable, modern family house. It truly was a fabulous grandma house, but they were not really in the market for a grandma house at this price, and the wrong decision would clearly impact their quality of life and their finances. While this house was really never a good fit for them, because they lacked experience, they did not see the difference between a well maintained home and an updated one, and it cost them over $700 in home inspection and sewer scope fees, not to mention costing them precious time.

So that you don't make the same mistake, part 2 of this book will help you learn some of the technical details necessary to compare, contrast, and describe the houses you see in the field, and part 3 will provide four ways to sort homes—by **owner**, **type**, **age**, and **style**—in order to apply this new vocabulary out in the real world.

HONING THE HOME INSPECTION FILTER: DISTINGUISHING MAJOR REPAIR CONCERNS FROM THE BONES

Several years ago, I had a client, Jolene, who wasted thousands of dollars on home inspections. It is not uncommon for me to provide multiple inspections for clients, particularly when home sales inventory is low. Low inventory sparks vigorous competition and often brings in multiple offers for a single house. When the market is like this, a home seller can have an open house on a Saturday and then say, "Okay, everyone, we will review your offers next Thursday. Good luck!"

The standard procedure in the Seattle area is to resort to the pre-offer consultation. This means buyers must get the home inspected *prior* to making their offer so that they can waive their inspection contingency, essentially saying to the seller, "We will take this house as is; we will not ask for any concessions or for anything to be repaired." The seller can then select whom they want to sell the house to, assured that everyone making an offer waived their inspection contingency.

This frantic and frustrating house-buying process can get expensive, and it can waste a lot of time and money. Many homebuyers end up paying for home inspections on multiple houses they don't get because, ultimately, someone else was willing to pay more for the house than they were. This type of hypercompetitive situation exists in hot markets throughout the country, taking different forms depending on the laws and standards of the state.

In Jolene's case, the first inspection I did was not a pre-inspection (she was under contract, which meant this was not a pre-inspection). It was a nice old house with good bones. It had an old, humble foundation but it had not settled much—a little over 1 inch in 100 years is not bad, and at least the foundation was all poured concrete. The siding was also humble, with some split and cracked siding boards, peeling paint, and a few places where wood rot required repair, but it was well protected by roof overhangs and so the repairs were not urgent. The house needed a bit of work, but for the most part one could pick away at the updates over time, and it was well within Jolene's price range so she would have some resources to work with on this house. In my mind, this seemed like an excellent house compared to other houses of similar age and type.

But a problem arose with two primary issues: rodents were getting into the attic and the roof required replacement. I tried to explain that rodent problems are quite common, and, though they can be pretty gross and a pain to deal with, you can often get professionals to clean, seal, and remediate for around $3,000. Replacing the roof is expensive but fairly straightforward: you get a few bids and you do it and you are done. Roof replacement is a major concern because it's expensive, maybe $6,000 on this house, but it's also a simple job—what I call a spread sheet item—and an owner can factor it into the cost of the house, put on the new roof and be done with it. When I asked my client if she had the financial flexibility to get a new roof, she said that she did but she was horrified at needing to put on a new roof and even more so at the thought of critters crawling around in the attic. Jolene could not get past these two findings, so she rescinded her offer.

Fast-forward to five home inspections later (on houses that all had multiple offers). Jolene had given up. She had quit looking for a house altogether and had decided to rent. Several of the other homes that we looked at were better than that first one, but she had gotten outbid. Several of the other homes were worse and she walked away without even making an offer. Maybe this worked out well for Jolene in the end; it's hard to know. But her dream of home ownership died when she was unable to get past the inspection discovery of some fairly typical repair work needed for a good little house.

LESSON LEARNED

If you don't want to miss out on a good house, you have to go about the house hunting process knowing that every home has problems. By organizing home systems into **core**, **entrenched**, and **disposable** categories, as this book discusses in part 2, you will learn about house systems with context so that you can distinguish whether a repair is expensive, complex, or routine. This critical context will help you take the information gleaned from a home inspection and put it through a filter of reality so that you can make sound and informed decisions. Know this: *There are no perfect homes.* When it comes to home repairs and maintenance, you need to decide which problems are worth fixing—or living with—and which ones are worth walking away from. "Pick your poison" is the old expression, and it aptly applies to making home-buying decisions.

Home inspectors and Realtors can help you with this, but ultimately these are decisions you make for yourself. Getting freaked out by routine types of maintenance can be just as expensive of a mistake as not recognizing deep dysfunction.

THE ART OF SEEING

At the age of 18, I was an avid hiker, and when I went away to college I left my familiar New England environs for the arid high deserts and mountains of Colorado. I loved hiking through the mountains, marveling at how different the world looked: rocks were red, trees were evergreen, and shrubs were scratchy beige, full of thorns and looked as though they could suck salt from the earth. I found the mountains and trails around my new home thrilling but also confusing; it was so stark and different that at times I felt as if I were walking across the surface of the moon.

My sophomore year in Colorado, I took a botany class. I commenced learning the trees, shrubs, and flowers of my new home. Putting names to the things I saw trailside began to transform my hikes.

What was even more interesting was the underlying context of the vegetation. I noticed that if I trod down to a mountain stream, I was likely to find pink elephant flower. If I found myself among a stand of lodgepole pine—a "fire-dependent species"—I was standing in an area that had had a forest fire in the not-too-distant past. Looking more closely, I could even see the fire-scorched stains on the rocks. The world around me was transformed by knowledge. Between my regular hikes and my botany and geology classes, I learned to see the world in a new light, and the moonscape I had apprehensively walked through upon my arrival became my playground.

The goal of *The Confident House Hunter* is to help you really "see" neighborhoods and homes in a new way, just as my botany and geology classes changed the way I saw the Colorado landscape. In the next chapter you will start your journey into developing a trained eye for looking at houses and understanding how to think about houses. We start with guiding principles. No technical details yet, just concepts, philosophies, and fundamental truths about houses and house hunting.

GUIDING PRINCIPLES **2**

Hindsight is 20-20, but foresight requires a prescription. To learn how to look at houses, your prescription is to study the guiding principles below to learn how to move beyond "looking" to "seeing" the bones of a home. If looking at homes was a spiritual practice, these guiding principles would be the mantras to be repeated daily.

Make these principles the magnifying glass through which you see every home before you make an offer. With practice, this new skill can become as automatic as jerking your hand away when you touch a hot stove.

As you read this chapter, remember that these sets of guiding principles are fundamental because they are at the core of looking at, sorting through, and thinking about houses, and therefore they are weaved throughout the rest of the book.

FOUR GUIDING PRINCIPLES ALL HOUSES SHARE

1. **All homes have shortcomings.** The trick to looking at homes is straightforward: compartmentalize problems. This will allow you to make accurate comparisons between homes and help remove emotion from the process. By understanding the difference between **core**, **entrenched**, and **disposable** systems, as is laid out in part 2 of this book, you will be better prepared to compartmentalize different problems and understand their importance. For example, a house that needs a new roof, new decks, and a new furnace may sound like a bad house, but it's not: those are

expensive systems but they are easy to install and they are disposable systems that often require updating anyway. By contrast, a
house with a bad foundation on a low lot with chronic drainage
problems and anobiid beetles in the framing below the house has
dysfunction in its bones and may be a good house to avoid.

2. **Simplicity is your friend.** While complex homes are not in any
way bad homes, they *are* more likely to be higher maintenance
homes. Higher maintenance costs can quickly break the family
budget. Compare it to owning a car: Some people own a Honda
Accord and others own a classic Jaguar. Most of us would rather
drive a Jag, but we want the maintenance record of an Accord.
You need to decide for yourself what type of home you want to
own, but when in doubt, remember that to minimize the cost of
maintenance and repair, simplicity is your friend.

3. **Water is the enemy.** At some point during home ownership,
nearly all homeowners encounter the fear that water is destroying their home. There is no more destructive force that works to
tear down your house than water. Plumbing, rain, groundwater,
condensation, and vapor all work to destroy a home; such forces
can lead to wood decay, mold, and wood-destroying organisms.
Controlling all of these forms of water is not easy. As a friend of
mine once said, "Water is some ornery stuff." Don't ever underestimate the power of water.

4. **Location. Location. Location.** Yes, it is the oldest real estate
cliché, but that's because it's true. To a home inspector, location
has less to do with the resale value of the lot and everything to
do with the lot's engineering characteristics. When you learn to
think critically about the location of the property you are looking
at, you'll be able to identify both benefits and potential problems.
Remember, there is one thing you cannot change: the lot location. A chronic problem caused by location is one of the most
difficult things to fix. If you buy a house on a steep, eroding
hillside or a lot that is difficult to access or at the bottom of a hill
by a swamp, these characteristics can impact the house and can
be difficult or even impossible to change. The piece of land you
are buying is at the very core of the asset that you call your home.

FIVE GUIDING PRINCIPLES FOR LOOKING AT HOUSES

1. **Know the history.** Understanding the history of the area in which you are looking to buy a house will help you understand the quality of the house. If the neighborhood was poor when the home was built, the house is more likely to be poorly built. If the neighborhood was wealthy when the home was built, you are more likely to be buying a nicely built house. You may be surprised to find pockets of nicely built older homes in lesser neighborhoods because the neighborhood has changed over time, often because a highway or airport was constructed nearby. By contrast, many older homes that were built by farmers or fishermen or as weekend beach houses were very poorly constructed but now stand in expensive neighborhoods that built up around them. People's expectations for these homes are often not in alignment with the house because the neighborhood is now nicer than the house. Dig into the history of neighborhoods where you are looking to buy a house to help guide you.

2. **Know local trends.** What are the types of houses and styles of houses in your target neighborhood that you can afford? What are the core systems of these houses like? Do they have slab foundations? Basements? Flat roofs? Learn the local building trends so you can more accurately compare and contrast homes. Be suspicious of homes with drastically different designs than what is prevalent—why didn't everybody build this way if it was such a great idea? Up here in the Pacific Northwest I am deeply suspicious of the flat-roofed stucco houses that look as though they migrated here from Los Angeles or Santa Fe. These buildings are so exposed to the weather that they tend to fare poorly in the wet Seattle climate.

3. **Rooflines matter.** The beauty, structure, and logic of a house begins at its roofline. If I had just one place to look to learn the most about a house, I would look at the roofline. Homes with dysfunctional rooflines are dysfunctional. Simple rooflines make simple houses. Beautiful houses have beautiful rooflines. Ugly houses have ugly rooflines. Houses with structural problems have sagging rooflines. Learn to look at rooflines as a quick trick to "see" houses.

4. **The 20-year rule.** The life cycle for many of the systems in our homes is roughly 15 to 20 years. Beware of the 20-year-old house or the house that had extensive remodel work done 20 years ago. These houses aren't bad, but know that houses that have not been updated in the last two decades are likely to need expensive systems maintenance and replacement. My "usual suspects" on a 20-year-old house are roof, deck, furnace, water heater, appliances, bathrooms, kitchen, and interior finishes such as carpets and paint. That's an expensive list. You will find tips for dating houses and systems in houses in chapter 9 of this book. This will help you to uncover and see the years of additions, repairs, and modifications that have been made to the house and better determine the amount of required maintenance looming ahead.

5. **Visualize the worst.** Imagine your prospective house in other conditions. If you are touring houses on a perfect early summer day, imagine what it would be like if it was pouring rain. In a snowstorm? A hurricane? During an earthquake? In the winter? In a strong wind? Always try to look at homes and visualize how they might perform when Mother Nature is at her worst. I am constantly amazed and terrified by how many more water problems I am able to find when I'm out inspecting during a hard driving rain: storm drains backing up, and water leaking into a basement or flooding a crawl space, for example. Bad weather is a good opportunity to see how a house holds up year-round.

THREE GUIDING PRINCIPLES FOR UNDERSTANDING AND MANAGING HOUSE PROBLEMS

1. **Core systems are key.** Your house is defined by its core systems: rooflines, location, orientation, site preparation and drainage, foundations, framing, access, and floor plan. They are the foundation of the built part of your investment. It is vital that you understand them. Learning the fundamentals of core systems and developing basic skills for looking at these systems will help you better contrast and compare problems uncovered during the home inspection. These are the systems a home inspector is looking at to see the bones beneath the bling, and they are discussed in chapters 4 and 5.

2. **Beware of the unknown.** Buying a house is an information-gathering process. The home inspection is one part of that process. However, one of the more frustrating things about being a home inspector is this: no matter how hard you try, you just cannot know everything there is to know about a house, especially from a limited visual inspection; there are too many important things in a house that are covered and obstructed from view. Think of the home inspection as halving the distance from the unknown to perfect knowledge; every additional inspection and round of research gets you that much closer to complete information. But remember, you will never reach perfection. *Perfect information does not exist in real estate.* You cannot eliminate risk; you can only hedge against it. Some homes have much greater risk than others, such as a flipped home where everything looks new and yet you don't really know the quality or scope of the work that was done behind the walls and finishes. So listen to your home inspector and remember: *Don't be afraid of what you know; be afraid of what you don't know.* An experienced home inspector won't just tell you what's wrong with the house; she or he will help you identify the risks so that you can decide if the next steps are worth taking.

Bad House/ Great Location

I once inspected a cottage style house in a great city neighborhood. It had a substandard foundation and 5 inches of settlement across the dining room: If you set a marble on the floor it would roll rapidly across the room without a push. It had been dressed up nicely so it was cute, small, (relatively) affordable, and in a great location. There was a lot of interest in this house. I didn't like it. This house was all about the bling and not the bones: It was essentially falling down.

When I looked at it, I saw a teardown. Even the real estate agent, Sue, acknowledged that it was a terrible house, but here's the irony: In 2006, Sue had a client who thought about buying a crappy house like this because it was in a great neighborhood. Sue's client instead bought a much nicer house in a lesser neighborhood. Fast-forward 8 years later: Sue tells me her clients are still underwater on the nice house they bought because it was located in a lesser neighborhood. Sad but true—they might have weathered the housing bubble better by buying the falling-down cottage in a great neighborhood.

23

3. **Look at the big picture.** There is more to diagnosing a real estate purchase than just assessing the condition of the building. The home inspection, while important, is just one piece of the puzzle. There is no substitute for having an experienced Realtor on your team to help you process and use the information gleaned from a home inspection, whether it's deciding that it's a house worth bidding on, negotiating with the seller for repairs or concessions, or encouraging you to walk away.

Remember that a home inspector is only looking at the condition of the building, not the price you are paying or the possibilities the future may hold. The Realtor will be able to ask more big-picture questions, such as, what if you have a double lot and a new light-rail station is proposed to go in a few blocks away? You could live in a lousy house for 5 years and then tear it down to build a duplex! These types of creative opportunities abound in real estate and a good Realtor can help you see them.

GETTING STARTED 3

Anybody can look at a house, but truly seeing is different from looking. Seeing implies some understanding about what is in front of you, and the goal of *The Confident House Hunter* is to move you from looking at houses to seeing them.

House System: An individual component of a house, such as roof covering, electric panel, furnace, window, or water heater.

The traditional approach to seeing houses, the one taught at home inspection schools, is to evaluate the systems that compose the house. When you look at a house, ask yourself: how old is each system? What needs to be repaired or replaced now, and what may require repair in the near future? By using a system-by-system method, you can logically break down a house as home inspectors do in their reports—by roofing, windows, decks, siding, heating and cooling, and so forth.

With a strong understanding of house systems, a good homeowner can develop a blueprint for house maintenance and updates. Homeowners with solid game plans for maintenance spend their maintenance dollars wisely. For example, if they know that they will need a new roof soon, they will hold off on the fancy kitchen remodel to ensure that critical maintenance is done first. When I inspect homes where owners have a firm grasp on their systems, the homes are updated in a logical sequence. By contrast, some of my least favorite homes are the ones with $100,000 kitchens on a failing foundation. . . . Yes, I do see houses like this.

The system-by-system method is also invaluable for comparing houses. If you are looking at two houses and one has all new systems except for an old clunky roof, and one needs lots of updating including new pipes, electrical work, bathrooms, kitchens, flooring, and a furnace, you can see that the house that needs the new roof will cost less to repair and update. Which house is right for you? Well, that depends on the prices of the houses, your budget, and your desires. Do you want a fixer project? Or do you want to just move into a house and do as little as possible?

Part 2 of this book will teach you what you need to know about house systems so that you are better prepared to see some of this for yourself when you are out looking at houses. This is a critical skill, which will help you see if a potential house is likely to meet your expectations. If you are not in the market for a fixer, develop skills for looking at house systems so that you can see for yourself if the house falls into this category or not. *This book will not replace a home inspection!* You cannot become an expert by reading a single book. But you will learn the average lifespan and replacement costs of many house systems and you will learn which house systems are complicated to repair and which ones are simple. These are the rudiments of learning to really see houses.

YOU NEED A SYSTEMS FILTER

Before we get started on technical stuff, you need to have a filter for understanding the complexity and cost associated with a house system. Most people would not mistake the cost of replacing a broken light with the cost of repairing a failing foundation. However, many people confuse the complexity of replacing a roof or a furnace with the complexity of correcting a chronic drainage problem or rewiring. Sometimes expensive but straightforward updates are more manageable to take on than a series of frustrating and complicated repairs that can have "the peeled onion effect": where you start to fix a piece of wood rot, which leads you to the flashing and then some siding and sheathing and then to the leaky gutter above and pretty soon you're tearing your whole house apart.

To help you better distinguish the different types of repairs you are likely to find and how important or complex they may be, this book will teach you about house systems in three categories: **core**, **entrenched**, and **disposable**.

Spend some time understanding these different categories and refer back to them frequently. They are the key to being able to learn about houses within a context. This is critical for both seeing houses *and* digesting the information you learn from your home inspector.

CORE, ENTRENCHED, AND DISPOSABLE SYSTEMS

Core Systems

- If executed well and performing correctly, core systems should last the life of the building.
- Repairs to core systems are needed when an important part of the house is "not performing as intended."
- Repairs to these systems are more likely to be complicated.
- Some homes with chaos in their core systems can be impossible to ever fully correct and may be the real stinkers you are trying to avoid.
- When repairing core systems, it's often difficult to distinguish where repairs begin and end.
- Houses with great core systems have great bones. Houses with problems in the core systems have problems in their bones.

Core Systems Include

- Rooflines
- Site: location, orientation, preparation, and drainage
- Foundation
- Framing
- Access
- Floor plan

Entrenched Systems

- Periodically need updating, but are more complex to update and more expensive than many basic repairs—often because these systems are behind wall and ceiling finishes.
- Can be more difficult to estimate repair and updating costs, often because of limited access and visibility.
- Homes with dysfunction in their entrenched systems are often great fixer houses—but not cosmetic fixers. These are the true fixers, where the best results are found in a cohesive remodel approach.

Entrenched Systems Include

- Siding
- Wiring

29

- Heating and cooling distribution
- Water piping systems
- Windows
- Insulation
- Ventilation

Disposable Systems

- In constant need of updating.
- Easy to update.
- Reliable replacement estimates are usually easily obtained for disposable systems.
- Houses that need nothing more than updated disposable systems are the ultimate cosmetic fixers.
- Not necessarily inexpensive. A new roof is expensive, but usually an easy project.

Disposable Systems Include

- Hot water heaters
- Heating and cooling equipment
- Roof coverings and skylights
- Gutters and downspouts
- Floor, wall, and ceiling finishes
- Exposed decks and porches
- Appliances
- Kitchens
- Bathrooms

LEARN TO DISTINGUISH BETWEEN EXPENSIVE REPAIRS, BASIC REPAIRS, AND COMPLEX REPAIRS

As you learn about house systems, remember that there are three types of systems repairs: expensive, basic, and complex. When you think about systems, remember this: If a system repair has a relatively certain price tag attached to it, then what we have is a cost, not a problem. Because it is a known quantity, you can assign a dollar figure to it and move on. If there are too many of these large dollar signs that get attached to a prospective house, you may decide to negotiate with the seller, or simply rescind your offer. You are now making an informed decision based on information. *This* is the objective of every home inspector: to help you make a decision based on information. Always keep this mantra in mind: Beware of the unknown—*in the world of looking at and understanding houses, I am never afraid of what I know; I am afraid of what I don't know.*

Expensive repairs are the big jobs, like replacing an old furnace or installing a new roof. A new roof could cost as much as $5,000 to $20,000 or more (depending on the size of the roof and the type of roofing material) and a new furnace is often in the $2,500 to $5,000 range. But replacing a roof is usually a simple project—you get three bids and you do it. Three days later, you're done. Don't mistake a house that needs an expensive update for a bad house. Purchasing a house that needs an expensive new roof is like buying a used car that needs an expensive set of new tires—it's just regular scheduled maintenance.

Basic repairs are ubiquitous in houses: a loose electric receptacle, a downspout that drains at the foundation, a cloudy window with a failed seal, a leaky kitchen sink faucet or drain. Expect that every house will require some amount of basic repair. If you are not handy, a long list of basic repairs can get expensive. One way to help think about cost for lots of small items is to lump them into full days or half days of labor. I use a local plumber who can get a remarkable amount of small tune-up plumbing work done in two hours.

Complicated repairs are my least favorite repairs, because they are hard to estimate. A leaking window that leads to rot below the frame is a great example. What at first appears simple quickly builds into a drawn-out investigation: Where exactly is the water coming from? How far into the building does the rot go? What will this look like when a contractor opens up the wall? Now compare a rot repair like this to a furnace replacement. A new furnace is a significant expense and having heat in your home is critical, but a furnace replacement is less likely to involve any surprises.

TIPS FOR DATING SYSTEMS IN HOMES

As you learn about systems, you are going to realize that the age of a system becomes important. Most of these systems don't last forever, so it's critical to get some idea of the various ages of certain things and how long they last. Some systems like siding and roofs are pretty tricky; there are no visible dates that you can read. Experienced home inspectors can often give you reliable "guestimates," but it can be hard to know for sure.

Other systems, like windows, hot water heaters, furnaces, toilets, and even Oriented Strand Board (OSB) sheathing can give you great clues as to the various ages of systems. This can be especially helpful in homes that have been added onto or remodeled so you can try and puzzle together the age of a remodel by looking in these places to find dates of manufacturer. Here are a few common places I look to find dates on systems in houses.

- In between double pane glass—not all windows have a date but many do (pictured top right).

- In water heaters and furnaces, look in the serial number. The date is often coded in the number, so for example, a serial number of GE 1004R13801 would indicate the appliance was manufactured in the tenth month of 2004 (pictured left).

- Refrigerators will sometimes have dates they were manufactured—this can help you date the age of a kitchen remodel.

- Permit stickers on electric panels (pictured bottom right).

- Inside toilet tanks—the date that the toilet was made can often be found there.

- On OSB sheathing, look for a stamp where you can often find a date. You might see this plywood visible in an unfinished garage or in the attic (pictured below).

YOU CAN LEARN THIS STUFF

You don't need to be a technical wizard to understand how to look at homes. In the following two chapters about core systems, you will discover the basic technical knowledge you will need to evaluate and understand these systems. Gaining a basic understanding of these systems is your first step in going from looking to seeing. This is your start in learning to avoid the emotional traps that besiege most homebuyers, because instead of noticing just the surface bling, you will start honing in on the systems of the house that a home inspector sees.

PART II

The Nuts and Bolts of Systems

CORE SYSTEMS I **4**

Understanding the core systems of a home is the key to learning how to "see" a home for what it really is. The core systems (listed on page 29) are at the heart of the question: "Does my house have good bones?" Houses with good core systems have good bones. Houses with dysfunctional core systems have problems with their bones.

As you read through the following systems chapters, it is important to remember that all houses have problems. It's also human nature to focus on the negative. Coupled with the fact that a home evokes one's strongest emotions, it's easy to talk yourself out of buying a home when you are overwhelmed by the prospect of house maintenance. My advice: Don't. Once you learn what to look for, and how to do so, you are prepared to hunt for a new home the right way. Understanding core systems is the vital first step to developing a filter for sifting through the myriad problems that arise during house hunting and home inspection so you can understand when to worry and what to do when house problems are discovered.

Also note that the systems section of this book, part 2, is the most technical part of this book. I know it can be hard to read about technical house stuff, but I have tried to boil down the information to the bare minimum that all homeowners should know. If you want to learn more, there are a lot of great books and resources available. The following chapters on systems should really be viewed as bare bones, must-understand knowledge if you are going to be a homebuyer or a homeowner.

ROOFLINES

As you will learn later in this book, the roof covering, such as your shingles, are simply an expensive disposable system, but what about the roofline? A roofline is defined as the outline or outer edge of a roof. The roofline should be the first thing you look for when touring houses. It is the first thing I look at. *There is no other single part of a house that can tell you more about a house in less time than the roofline.*

The roofline will determine the shape of the space that is weathered-in (enclosed) below: your floor plan. The roofline dictates the exposure of your siding, windows, and doors. It defines how your building will shed water and deflect damaging UV rays. Learning to look critically at rooflines is a skill that is often overlooked, but the average homebuyer can learn how to do it without any technical training, it just takes some basic knowledge and a desire to learn how to look.

Let's look at the illustrations for the various types of roofline designs and varying pitches. This is important vocabulary so you can describe the rooflines you see.

Sloped Roof Shapes

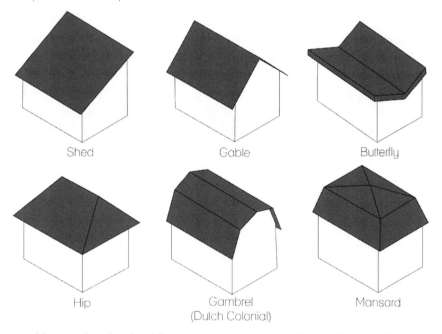

In addition to these sloped roof shapes, there is the low slope or flat roof. Courtesy of Carson Dunlop, copyright 2016©, www.carsondunlop.com.

About Roof Pitches

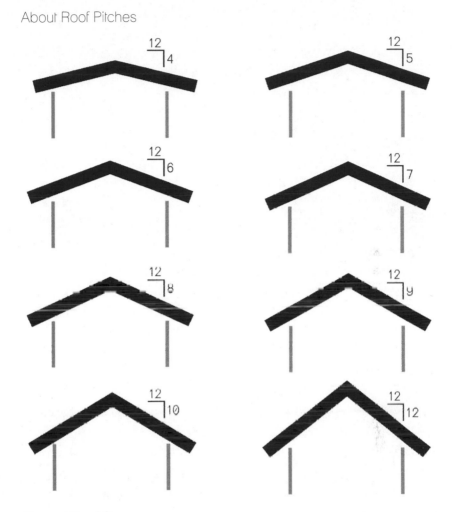

Sloped Roof Shapes

How a roof slopes is often referred to as its pitch. Roof pitches are measured as a function of the slope (also called "fall") over the run. For example, a 5/12 roof will fall 5 inches over a 12-inch run. This is also critical vocabulary for being able to describe what you see.

How to Look at Rooflines

To look at a roofline, start by stepping back from the house and observing at a distance. Take in what you see. Does the house look sturdy? Complicated? Simple? Elegant? Vulnerable? Weak? Does it look as though the roof will shed water reliably in a hard rain or will it pool and become trapped? Does it appear as though additions have been done or is this an original roofline? Are there large roof overhangs to protect the siding or does the roof leave the rest of the home exposed to the weather? Can you even see a roofline or is it a flat roof with no real roofline?

This house lacks overhangs, exposing the building to the weather. Expect higher maintenance costs and shorter service life for siding, windows, doors, and trim.

Once you take in this bigger picture, move closer and try to orient yourself to the roofline so you can sight your eye along the plane of the roof and the ridge. This is not always possible without a ladder—it depends on how the house is sitting on the lot. What do you see? Do you see dips and sags in the roofline? If you do,

Expect water to pool on flat roofs because they don't slope to drain well. You may need a ladder to see the condition of a flat or low slope roof.

that can indicate structural weakness. Do you see large humps? These can indicate an addition or perhaps structural problems.

You do not need to be a home inspector to see this. Keep in mind  that many older homes have some moderate sagging in the roof frame, but extensive sagging is a red flag. Sags and dips should be noted and pointed out to your home inspector for further evaluation. You can also go inside the house and see if you can find similar sagging patterns there.

Compare the rooflines of these two homes. Notice how the top one sags compared to the sturdy roofline below.

DYSFUNCTIONAL ROOFLINES

Dysfunctional rooflines are those that simply don't make sense. Think for example of a roof that drains toward the side of the house. Does the roofline look logical to you or is it odd? Does it look as though the roofline was designed? Or does it look as though a group of alien spaceships have landed on the house? Be wary of homes with dysfunctional rooflines because they belie an underlying dysfunction to the whole house. Houses with dysfunctional rooflines are complicated houses or hodgepodge houses that have had many additions over the years.

These homes have dysfunctional rooflines as a result of remodels. Dysfunctional rooflines are often dysfunctional houses.

FLOOR PLAN ROOFLINES

Floor plan rooflines are where sections of the roof drain toward the siding or large sections of the roof drain right into a small piece of gutter. I see these rooflines on many new big houses as well as modern townhouses. Why in the world would you drain your roof at the side of your house?

These modern townhomes have a floor plan roofline with roofs draining into tiny gutters—they may not shed water efficiently and gutter leaks could run down the side of the building.

ELEGANT AND PRACTICAL ROOFLINES

Elegant rooflines have grace, charm, and utility. From a practical side, I love the $5/12$ pitch. This is steep enough to shed water well, but not so steep that you cannot walk on and service the roof. You can also build nice roof overhangs on a house with a $5/12$ roof pitch.

If you have a roof with a steep $12/12$ pitch you will shed water well and the roof may last a long time, but large overhangs will create a dark house because the overhanging roof will shade the windows. Most homes with steep roof pitches do not have good overhangs to protect the building. The pitch will also be too steep to walk on it safely, making it difficult to service the roof.

Houses with low-slope rooflines can feature great roof overhangs that do not block out as much light, but a low-slope does not shed water as well and you should expect a roof membrane system necessitating more maintenance at greater costs. Compare this to a more simple shingle system on a sloped roof—this will require less maintenance, costing you less.

From a maintenance standpoint, a flat roof with a big roof overhang that protects the siding can be a good trade-off; think of this as a high-maintenance roof for low-maintenance siding.

However, when you have a house with a flat roof and no overhangs, you have a structure that is very exposed to the weather. When it rains, the siding and windows get wet and the roof may not shed water well. In general, these structures are best suited to desert climates. In such a structure, I would expect higher maintenance costs for entrenched systems such as siding, decks, and windows as well as the roof.

Floor Plan Roofline

I recently inspected one during a brisk rain. The roof drained toward the wall of the house and the valley between the roof and the siding was clogged up with debris, so water was running down the side of the house. The house was just 10 years old. When I crawled underneath this wet section of wall in the crawl space I found moisture ants (see more on moisture ants in chapter 14) and water damage. The result: extensive parts of the adjoining wall were going to have to be torn apart and rebuilt. The architect may have designed a floor plan that the buyer liked, but the roof design was vulnerable and lack of maintenance combined with a vulnerable design led to an expensive water damage problem after only 10 years.

ROOF OVERHANGS ARE YOUR FRIEND

I really can't say enough about the value of good roof overhangs. These are like an umbrella for your house. They deflect damaging UV rays and wind-driven rain. I will sometimes see homes that are 100 years old and the original siding that is protected by a generous roof overhang is still in excellent condition. On the other hand, roofs with no roof overhangs could require extensive siding and window repairs as often as every 20 or 30 years.

The siding under this large roof overhang could last 100 years.

HOME ADDITIONS

One of the most frequently asked questions homebuyers ask is, "Can we add an addition?"

My answer is virtually always the same: Think about how an addition will affect the roofline.

As long as you have enough land and you are in compliance with local building regulations regarding setbacks to neighboring properties, you can almost

This disjointed roofline is likely to be higher maintenance and have a shorter useful service life and be more expensive to replace because of all the odd angles and details.

always add onto a house. To make sure it has a positive or neutral impact on the existing home, it's all about how it will affect the roofline. That is the key question.

SITE LOCATION

Location. Location. Location. Overcoming a poor site location is difficult. Whether a busy road, a loud airport, a nearby prison, a swampy lot, a dark lot, a steep eroding hillside, or a hillside prone to forest fires, all of these scenarios can be difficult to repair or engineer your way around.

Despite what the county tax assessor may tell you, the single most valuable thing you are buying in real estate may be the land and where it is located. You can tear down a structure and build a new one, but you can't move the plot of land underneath your home.

You do not need to be a technical expert to critically evaluate your site location and think about how this might impact your house.

Ten No-brainer site conditions to look for

1. Look for hillsides and critical slopes that could endanger the house or lead to seasonal drainage problems. If you are concerned about these, you may want to hire a geotechnical engineer or soils engineer to further investigate the property for you. A geotech can often provide very specialized information about the local geology of your region. One geotech I have worked with uses geologic maps with the streets on top so he can tell you exactly what type of soils your house is sitting on and educate you about the characteristics of the specific soils.

Ugly Buildings

Early in my construction career, I was working within earshot of a generally well regarded architect. I was impressed by his sense of style and enjoyed the homes he designed. One day, I found an opportunity to ask him a question that had perplexed me:

"Why are there so many ugly buildings?" I asked.

He looked at me, smiled, then thought for a moment and he said, "People design floor plans, they don't design rooflines." Then he walked away, looking rather pleased with his answer.

I am not sure if he made this up or simply passed along conventional architect wisdom, but his words echo in my head. When you tour homes, it will start resonating in yours if you are looking carefully. The roofline is one of the most important bones of a house. Dysfunctional rooflines can be impossible to repair, and beautiful, functional rooflines can be difficult to replicate. Rooflines are the first place I start when looking for clues about the structure, design, and quality of a home.

2. Look for nearby rivers or streams that could flood during heavy rains.

3. Look for plants growing that could indicate a wet lot—most regions of the country have plants endemic to streams, creeks, and bogs. For example, in the Seattle area, I look for horsetail—a plant that tells me the soils get very wet at least seasonally.

4. Does the driveway or nearby streets slope toward the house?

5. Is the lot very flat? This can lead to seasonal standing water and a high water table.

6. Is the lot exposed to lots of wind?

7. Is this house in an area prone to forest fires? Floods? Earthquakes?

8. Is there vegetation growing too close to the home that could trap water against the house or create rodent cover?

9. Are there large trees near the house that may present safety hazards and require expensive tree work?

10. Are there sinkholes around the property that could indicate poor site work and risks for ongoing settlement?

SITE ORIENTATION

One important characteristic of a house that is often overlooked by homebuyers is the home's orientation to the sun.

Guiding Principles of Orientation

- **Southern sun is your friend.** When the sun is low in the horizon in the winter, this will give you light and passive heat. In the summer, when the sun is traveling much higher in the sky, the sun will no longer beat directly into these windows.

- **Western sun can cook you** and lead to more need for cooling. Hot western sunsets can shine those UV rays directly into your house. Consider blinds for the windows for summertime sun.

- **Eastern sun is your friend.** Usually cooler in the morning, it can be nice to have morning eastern light.

- **Northern light can be great** in skylights and clerestory windows: Passive filtering light can make for lovely interior light.

Four House Orientation Tips

1. When touring homes, see how the light comes: Are you buying a "light house" or a "dark house"?

Let There Be (Sun)light

I once moved into this terrific, dilapidated little beach house that had a fantastic western view of the mountains and sunset. On the first beautiful hot summer day, we invited friends over for dinner; we nearly perished on the patio as the western sun cooked us like hamburgers—I just had not thought about how this little place would perform on a hot summer day

2. Rooms with windows on more than one face of a wall will create nicer light—as will skylights and clerestories. Corner windows can create a great panoramic effect, especially in homes with views.

3. Note that in many climates, exposure to southern and western aspects will create higher maintenance costs for siding, decks, and windows due to wind, rain, and UV exposure. This could change regionally depending on microclimate conditions in your area. What are the aspects in your region that are higher maintenance? These are the sides of the building to go looking for problems on the outside of the house.

4. Even if you are looking at a house on a perfect sunny spring day, try to imagine the house in a driving rain and on a dark winter night.

SITE PREPARATION

If you build a house today, there is a good chance that the single most expensive line item in your construction budget is site preparation. Think of site preparation as earth moving: digging out the foundation, sloping adjacent soils away from the house, installing drainage, and creating level areas where there was once hillside. Site preparation employs expensive earth-moving equipment and there is often a lot of gray area regarding how far a builder will go to prepare a site for the house. For this reason, it is common to see inadequate or marginal site work.

Neat Historical Context: When looking at older homes it is valuable to think about the tools that people had to build those homes. Today's beautiful diesel-powered CAT and backhoe equipment were not available in older times, meaning site preparation today is generally better than it used to be. Put yourself in your city in 1900 or 1920 and go build a foundation—what tools would you be using? A lot of older homes, you will look at will have hand-dug foundations. In some parts of the country, you may find fieldstones or rubble foundations. Expect much more humble foundations in homes prior to the 1940s.

Site Work to Look For

1. Look at the grade of the property—is it sloping toward the building or away from it? Ideally, all soils are sloped to drain away from the house. One technique for this is a swale.

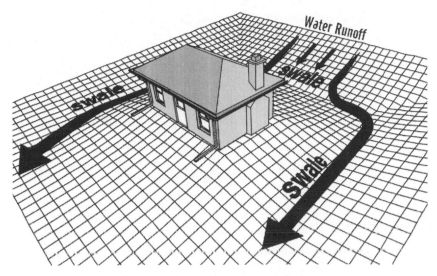

Courtesy of Carson Dunlop, copyright 2016©, www.carsondunlop.com.

2. Determine if the wood frame of the house is above grade. Good construction will lift the home nicely above grade—6 inches is modern code. Houses with wood too close to the ground are more vulnerable to wood destroying organisms.

The back side of this house is below grade—inadequate site work on an old house.

3. Are there retaining walls that are leaning, cracking, rotting, incomplete, or missing?

4. Are there soils sloping toward or sloughing against the house?

5. Is the crawl space nicely excavated or does it have marginal clear-

ances between framing and soils. Marginal clearances make a home less valuable; it's harder to access a house like this for inspections and repairs and the wood frame is more vulnerable to wood destroying organisms.

SITE DRAINAGE

Site drainage can be difficult to evaluate, especially during a dry time of year. You should always be thinking of what conditions could be like on your site in different weather conditions. Below you will find helpful tips of things to look for and some critical terms to understand about houses and site drainage.

WHAT SHOULD I LOOK FOR?

- If it is an older building, look to see if the visible drainpipes have been updated. Do you see plastic pipes that would not be characteristic of older building materials? Do you see catch basins or sump pumps installed? Do downspouts just terminate to grade, indicating no real drainage system? Updates or repairs to the drainage system of a house usually indicate prior problems—people don't add new plastic drainpipe or sump pumps just for fun.

- Look for old storm drainpipes made from clay or concrete tiles. I am always a bit suspicious of pipes that have been in the ground for 100 years. . . . What are the odds that these pipes are clogged or partly clogged?

- Even newer plastic drainpipes can fail. These corrugated pipes are not well suited to below grade drainage and are often clogged, crushed, and backed up.

- If the downspouts are discharging into drainpipes in the ground, do you see washed out soil around them as though they are backing up or clogged? You can look for a "tide line" on the base of the downspout where it enters the storm drain—this would tell you there has been standing water in the drain and it has been backing up.

- Are the downspouts discharging adjacent to the house? Getting roof runoff as far away from the house as possible is the best practice and critical to keeping the building dry and preventing settlement.

- If it has a finished basement, look for signs of waterproofing. Beware of newly finished basements in old homes with no waterproofing. Remember when an old basement was built, there was likely little to no waterproofing done.

- If you can see the basement walls, look for white mineralization or efflorescence. This is like a sweat stain left on your tee shirt and can indicate prior moisture or dampness.

- If it has a crawl space, look for water or tide-lines in the crawl space or water stains that could indicate prior moisture problems. Is there a sump pump in the crawl space?

- Look at the vegetation growing on your lot: Do you see plants that look like they grow in wet soils? What could this mean about seasonal drainage?
- Look around the neighborhood: What was it like before it was built on? A field? A forest? A wetland? A plateau? Are you situated on what might have been an old creek? Research is your friend. It's time to be observant and play detective.
- Many driveways slope toward the garage. See if drainage has been installed near the garage to collect runoff.
- Look at the city street and make sure it is not draining onto your property. Imagine a heavy downpour: Will the drainage from a city street run right at your house?
- Look in basement stairwells: Does it look like water is pooling here?

DRAINAGE: UNDERSTANDING DIFFERENT DRAINS

The following will give you some basic vocabulary and knowledge about different types of drainage pipes and configurations, but with a word of warning. I find that contractors, builders, Realtors, and home inspectors confuse a number of these terms and some of this terminology varies regionally. Do not feel frustrated if you get a bit confused or need to ask a professional to explain exactly what they mean by a certain type of drainage.

Footing Drain: This drain is installed at the base of foundation footings. If installed correctly in a trench below your footings, this will collect

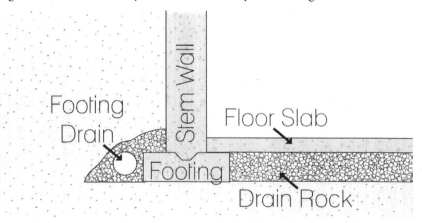

Courtesy of Carson Dunlop, copyright 2016©, www.carsondunlop.com.

groundwater and keep a basement or crawl space dry by putting your house up on a pedestal. Footing drains are tricky to install well. They must be at the right depth with the correct slope to intercept ground water. You will never see a footing drain—they are below ground. Most old buildings do not have footing drains; this is the primary reason why old buildings are more prone to basement and crawl space moisture problems. These are also sometimes referred to as foundation drains.

Interior Drain: Similar to a footing drain but installed inside the house and cut into a basement floor slab. These are often used by basement waterproofing contractors to waterproof a wet basement.

Curtain Drain: This type of drain is usually installed above a house on a hillside and wraps around a house in an attempt to intercept groundwater before it gets to your house. Such drains are generally ditches filled with gravel and perforated pipe—perforations facing down—to collect and divert ground water. Curtain drains are also tricky to install well; they must be set at the right depth to intercept ground water. It is generally more reliable to install a footing drain because the pipe should be below your foundation footings.

Infiltration Pit: A below-grade pit, usually filled with gravel so that collected drainage water will run into the ground. These are also sometimes referred to as French drains.

Daylighting: A drainpipe that runs below ground and exits through the visible end of the pipe. These are my favorite because you can check them to ensure they are performing correctly.

Tight-line: A solid pipe that runs below ground to pick up roof runoff from the ends of downspouts, diverting the water away from a building. These are sometimes called storm drains or downspout drains.

CONCLUSIONS ON CORE SYSTEMS I

You are starting to learn the building blocks to answer the question: does this house have good bones? I hope that this information is already starting to transform how you look at and think about houses. Remember that all problems are fixable. If you see problems with some of these things in your perspective house, it does not make it a bad house. *Every house is a great house for the right person at the right price.* However, problems with core systems are generally more complicated, expensive, and difficult to rectify than other systems in a house.

CORE SYSTEMS II **5**

The entire investment you are making in your house rests, quite literally, on the foundation.

Materials and techniques for building foundations vary regionally. Smart research will include learning the foundations that are common in your part of the country and understanding their relative strengths and weaknesses. Below is a list of common foundation configurations and materials.

FOUNDATION CONFIGURATIONS

House foundations come in three basic configurations:

1. Basements
2. Crawl spaces
3. Slab on grade

Many houses will have just one of these configurations, but some homes could have all three. Inherent to each of these configurations are some advantages and disadvantages.

Basements

PRO: Basement configurations have the obvious plus of more square footage and useful bonus/storage space. Basements are also dug deeper into the ground so footings for the foundation are deeper and more likely to be resting on stable, well compacted soils; thus I find homes with basements are generally less prone to structural settlement compared to homes with crawl spaces and slabs. You tend to see more basement configurations in cold climates where you have to dig down below frost level for footing systems.

CON: Basements are prone to moisture problems, especially if they have not been well waterproofed. Because the basement is "inside" your living space, even minor moisture problems in a basement can affect indoor air quality and damage your finishes or belongings.

Crawl Spaces

PRO: Crawl spaces are less expensive to build because you have less excavation costs and lower concrete costs. Also, if you have a drainage problem with a crawl space, the space is technically "outside" the building and often vented to the outdoors, so these configurations are more tolerant of minor moisture conditions.[1]

CON: It is common to find a litany of problems in crawl spaces. Expect to find something to repair in the crawl space—including structural problems, rodents, wood destroying organisms, plumbing leaks, and drainage problems. Also, the footings in a crawl space configuration are not as deep as a basement, so the home may be more prone to settlement. For example, a lot of old buildings are part basement and part crawl space and you will find the crawl space side often settles relative to the more stable and deeper basement side.

Slabs on Grade

PRO: The primary advantage of a slab on grade foundation is simplicity. This is just a big slab of concrete and there is no space below to repair. Slab foundations are very common in dry desert climates where the soils stay dry.

---

1. In some parts of the country, encapsulated crawl spaces may be prevalent. This is when the crawl space is not vented to the outdoors. See more on this in chapter 7.

CON: The disadvantages to slab on grade foundations are that there is nowhere to run new piping and wiring, so access is limited if you need to update systems. Also, if a slab has moisture problems, it can be difficult to correct. Slab on grade foundations have footings closer to grade so settlement can be an issue, especially in places where they have problems with expansive soils.

FOUNDATION MATERIALS

Foundations are constructed from a wide variety of materials. The list below starts with the strongest materials and concludes with the weakest. There is some subjectivity here, including the location of the house, the presence of seismic activity, and the quality of the installation, but these are reliable guiding principles.

1. **Modern Poured Concrete:** The strongest, best reinforced, and most water-resistant.
2. **Old Poured Concrete:** A good strong foundation but likely less reinforced and often on a site that is not as well prepared as a modern foundation.
3. **Concrete Block (CMU):** Great foundations in parts of the country without seismic risk. Older CMUs are usually not seismically reinforced. CMU foundations are porous and difficult to waterproof well.

Compare this sturdy modern poured concrete foundation to the post system pictured below.

4. **Brick/Stone:** Not well suited to areas with seismic activity. Some quality specimens exist in older parts of the country, such as New England.
5. **Post and Pier:** Visualize the house resting on wooden posts. The frame is often concealed by a skirting system but structurally

they are not too different than a deck. Seismically weak and nearly impossible to rodent-proof, these foundations are indicative of cottage style construction.

IMPORTANT STRUCTURE TERMS

Before we dig deeper into foundations, here are two terms you will need to understand:

- **Spread Footing:** The wide portion below the concrete stem wall that is wider than the foundation stem wall. Footings are often not visible.
- **Stem Wall:** The part of the foundation one can see—the stem wall is the concrete wall that extends above the ground, and on which the wood frame of the building is installed.

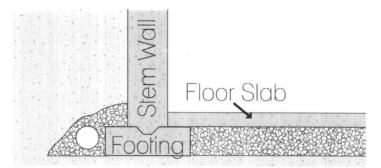

Courtesy of Carson Dunlop, copyright 2016©, www.carsondunlop.com.

Now let's explore some common questions about foundations, starting with one of the most basic questions.

Q: Why do houses settle?

A: The simple answer is that the soils below the foundation are not adequately supporting the weight of the building.

Let's think of foundations in three parts, with the first two being most critical.

1. **The Soils below the Foundation:** Ideally, the soils below the foundation are solid, stable, dry, and compacted. The entire house is resting on the soils below the house. Houses constructed on unstable soils are likely to be unstable houses.

   • Houses built on hillsides are prone to differential settlement because the half of the house that is cut into the hillside is on well compacted soils and the downhill side of the house may be on less compacted soils or even fill. This is called a cut-and-fill lot.

Notice how the builder cut into the hillside to build this house.

   • Houses built in parts of the country where there is an extensive annual freeze and thaw cycle can be prone to foundation problems as the soils freeze, expand, and heave below the house. Footings in these climates need to be installed adequately below the frost depth.

- Other parts of the country suffer from expansive soils. These areas have clay particulate in the soils that expand and contract as the soils get wet and then dry out. These seasonal expansions can exert uplift forces as much as 5500 pounds per square foot on a foundation.

Additional potential soil problems that can be regional include sinkholes and critical slopes (hillsides prone to sliding). Understanding common soil conditions in your area can help you learn to look for these problems as you are touring houses. If you are concerned about a prospective home's soils problems, consider hiring a soils engineer or geotech to get specific advice about the soils on and around the property.

2. **The Spread Footing:** This is the part of the foundation that rests directly on the soils. The classic problem in older buildings is small, inadequate footings resting on poorly prepared soils. In some buildings you may also see undermining, where parts of the foundation have no bearing soils at all below parts of the foundation.
3. **The Stem Wall:** This is the part of the foundation you typically see. Cracks in a stem wall are not usually the cause of a structural problem but a symptom indicating inadequate soils or footings that are causing settlement and stress in the concrete.

Q: Are new foundations better than old foundations?

A: While there are exceptions to every rule with houses, the reality is that new foundations are much more likely to be better than old foundations. I think of "new" foundations as being 1970s and newer, middle-age foundations are 1940s to 1960s, and then old are older than 1940s. There are several reasons why new foundations are often better:

1. The site work today is done with large earth-moving equipment. Imagine excavating a foundation site in 1902 with shovels and pick axes. Today's homes have better prepared sites on which to build.
2. Today we have much better procedures and standards for reinforcing concrete and for building concrete foundations. When building a foundation today, the city's building officials should inspect the walls for reinforcing rebar prior to pouring the

foundation to ensure they have been correctly reinforced.

Q: How much cracking is too much?

A: As a finger-to-the-wind guiding principle, cracks smaller than ¼ of an inch wide are typical in poured concrete. Remember, concrete is a rigid material that loves to crack. There is no need to become hysterical over small cracks in concrete. Cracks larger than ¼ of an inch are more of a red flag. Look for signs of fresh cracking. Fresh-looking concrete in a crack is indicative of recent movement. Fresh cracks will have a bright color to them with sharp edges. Old cracks have a worn, dull appearance, rounded edges, and may not have moved for many years. Another tip is looking for displacement in the crack, where the two sides of the crack have moved relative to each other.

Factoid

Believe it or not, the city of Seattle did not start requiring a permit to build a foundation until the mid-1960s! Hard to know if anybody was checking to see if older foundations were built correctly.

Q: What if I see large cracks in the concrete slab of a garage or in a basement?

Left: Very large foundation crack. This is a red flag that indicates structural settlement. Expect expensive repairs. Right: Typical moderate crack. Cracks like this one are common on older poured concrete foundations.

A: Cracks in concrete slabs—on the floor of a garage for example—are common. Your concrete slab is *not* part of the structure—it is the footings and the stem wall that support the house and the slab is just poured in the middle. You commonly find exposed concrete slabs in garage floors and unfinished basement floors. Sometimes cracks in the floor slab can be indicative of settlement but often they are not, especially in old basements where the concrete was just thrown down and poorly prepared soils below leave uneven floors. I would follow any cracks to the stem wall and look for cracking in the foundation wall or other signs of settlement. Even extreme cracks in floor slabs are not necessarily structural if no other signs of settlement can be found. They could be expensive to repair if you want a level floor surface but unless there are other signs of settlement in the building, the floor slab can settle without impacting the structure of the house.

Q: What are control joints?

A: Control joints are the lines you see that get cut into concrete during the original pour—think of the lines in a sidewalk. By installing control joints, you allow a place for the concrete to crack that does not damage the surface of the concrete. Many places like garage and basement slabs do not employ control joints, thus you see cracks forming in the field of the floor.

Q: Why would a house continue to settle after the weight of the building should have compressed the soils below the foundation?

A: The most common cause of on-going settlement in older buildings is lack of water control. Remember this: *Wet soils do not bear weight well. Dry compacted soils do.* That's why it is important that the roof and site runoff is directed away from the house and the foundation.

Q: Can I remodel a house with structural problems?

A: Yes, but . . . while renovating an old house can be fun and rewarding, make certain you are renovating a building that is sitting on a sound foundation and has a sound structure. The time to make structural repairs to a house is *before* you begin your face-lift—not after. Don't put lipstick on a pig. Throwing on a new coat of paint and adding new finishes to a house with structural problems is delaying the inevitable, and it shows a lack of understanding about houses and updating.

Q: Why do I need permits for structural changes?

A: One of my structure contractor friends likes to say, "Nobody can see what I do." This is very true. If structural modifications have been made to the home, there is often no way to look at the house and know if it was done correctly. Structural repairs and modifications should be permitted to protect the homeowner and future homebuyers.

RED FLAGS FOR STRUCTURES

When it comes to looking for structural red flags, you need to know that many older homes exhibit some of these symptoms. If you are looking at homes built prior to the 1940s, you should not try and take this list and assume that you will find a house that has no structural red flag of any kind; if you do, you will look at a lot of houses before you find one that is structurally perfect. However, these tips do give you the knowledge you need to look critically at house structures.

The goal here is to enhance your confidence and comfort when looking at houses so you are more aware and better prepared for the home inspection. Take what you see for yourself and bring your list of questions and observations to your home inspection—this will help you get more from your home inspection. It should also make house hunting more fun and less intimidating.

The Paper Trail

I was inspecting an upscale home in a wealthy neighborhood in Seattle. The house had a beautiful view of a lake and was perched on a steep hillside above a ravine. The house had clearly settled into the ravine. The seller, in their disclosure statement, said that their cousin had done pin-piling work, assuring a potential buyer that the house was now structurally sound. (Pin pilings are piers driven deep into the ground until they meet resistance from stable soils—then you attach the foundation to these pilings.) Unfortunately, the cousin had not pulled permits for the work nor was it engineered—there was no paper trail. Even if the work was done adequately, the seller had absolutely no way to prove it. The structural work that was done was worthless from a resale perspective.

Tip: When looking at the structure, learn to "sight" your eyes along surfaces. This necessitates moving your eyes into a position where you have perspective. If you want to see if a chimney is plumb[2] and not leaning, get your eyes into a position where you can "sight" the chimney.

Structural Red Flags to Look For

- Forty-five degree cracks in window and door headers or masonry wall assemblies (pictured on the following page)
- Cracks in hard floor surfaces such as tile (pictured on the following page)

---

2. Plumb means perfectly vertical.

- Foundation cracks larger than ¼ of an inch or stair step cracks in block foundations or brick siding
- Floors that are not level and walls that are not plumb. Look for old masonry chimneys that are leaning
- Doors that do not close or windows that are crooked
- Doors that have been planed down to fit into the door frame and trapezoidal door openings

Often straight line cracks that follow sheetrock seams are not indicative of settlement, but poor workmanship or shrinkage. If a house was built in the winter when the wood was wet, it could shrink up quite a bit as it dries out. If a house was framed quickly, there could be some framing that was not well installed and has created a weak point, causing cracks along a sheetrock seam. You might also see nail pops where nails are protruding from the sheetrock—this is common in newer construction, especially on the second floor, and often the result of seasonal expansion and contraction of the roof frame.

Q: What about the fixer house with structural problems?

A: Sometimes, finding a house with structural problems can be a good deal. If the property has languished on the market because people were afraid of these problems and you can implement a plan to repair the problems, you can create value. The problem: This type of repair is tricky and risky and best done during a more extensive renovation to the house. Tackling structural problems and extensive renovations are projects best suited for experienced contractors or homebuyers with experience and risk tolerance.

Q: What are the different ways foundations get repaired?

A: Foundations can be repaired in many ways. Here are three common solutions:

1. **Pin Pilings:** Pilings are driven into the ground until they meet resistance and then they are attached to the foundation to prevent ongoing settlement. The number of pilings and the depth they are driven to is determined by an engineer.

Pile Foundations

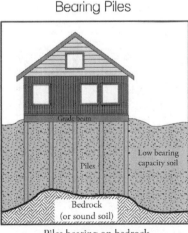
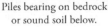
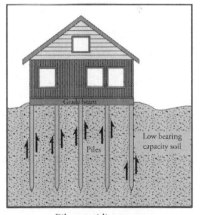

Bearing Piles	Friction Piles
Piles bearing on bedrock or sound soil below.	Piles providing support through skin friction.

Pile systems are not always used to repair. This is a diagram of a building engineered with a piling system. Courtesy of Carson Dunlop, copyright 2016©, www.carsondunlop.com.

The top of a pin piling, which is repairing a failing foundation.

2. **Adding to and Improving the Spread Footings:** This is done when the spread footing system for the house is inadequate. Repair involves giving the foundation a better footing system in a localized area such as a problematic corner.

3. **Lifting the House to Install a New Foundation:** Believe it or not, there are companies that can completely lift a house and put it on a new foundation; they can even move it down the street or across town if you like. Before you do this, be certain the house is worthy of such an investment. This is a *huge* project.

FRAMING

Poorly executed house framing can be hard to spot; especially if you can't see the framing and you are not a specialist. Framing and structure can feel confusing and intimidating. So relax and use your powers of observation. You do not need to be a contractor or an engineer to look critically at framing and structure—at least in a way that helps you be better prepared for the home inspection.

One thing to remember about looking at house structure is it is rare to see just one thing that explains what is happening to a house structurally. I note things as I go and connect the dots as I progress through my inspection. For this reason, the simple act of being aware can be helpful. Don't expect to see one thing and understand what is happening to the house structurally. It's okay to not understand. The simple fact that you are "seeing" is often enough to make you more educated and aware. Here you will find pointers of where to really look for house structure clues.

7 Tips for Looking at House Framing

1. **Do you see sags or dips in the roof frame?** Sight your eyes along the roofline. This is where I take my first clues about the structure of the house. Run your eyes along the roofline—look at the ridge and then sight the slope of the roof, looking for excessive dipping and sagging. If it is an old house, some amount of sagging is normal, but it should  not be excessive. You should point out your observations to your home inspector. If sagging is severe, consider looking for a different house or enlisting professional engineering services for their opinion.

2. **Do the floors slope inside the house?** Though most old homes have sloping floors, you need to be aware of them and think of three primary things:

    - Examine where the slopes are and how they could impact your daily life: Will you need to shim your furniture? Will a chair at the dining room table sit at an angle? This is important because this is what you are buying.
    - You also want to see how badly floors are sloping to determine how much movement has occurred. This is subjective, but 1 inch or less is very common in older homes and often no big deal. More than 2 inches can start to be

problematic for placing furniture, especially more than 2 inches across one room. Significantly more than 2 inches across one room is indicative of structure problems that may require repair.

- Most important, you want to try and determine if any repairs are required to prevent ongoing movement in the building. Such a determination may require a specialist. Have your home inspector take a first look, but a qualified general contractor or an engineer may be needed. If you are going to need to make structural repairs, you want to see if you can improve the structure and at least partly level out the building during repairs.

Note: It can sometimes be difficult to remove settlement from a building more than 1 to 2 inches unless you are undertaking more extensive renovations. Once old buildings have settled, it can be traumatic to shove them too far back into place because this can cause windows and doors to crack and bend and walls and ceiling finishes to crack.

3. **Do the floors slope around the chimney?** This is not usually a framing issue, but a sign of settlement in the house relative to the chimney. When floors slope down to the chimney, it indicates that the chimney is sinking or has sunk. If the floors slope away from the chimney, the house is settling relative to the chimney. In either case, repairs to the house or chimney might be necessary.

4. **Do the floors slope around the stairs?** The stairs are generally the weakest point in the floor frame system. This is because a large hole was cut into the floors when the stairs were built. If this was not done correctly, the framing will sag around the stairs.

5. **Are the floors bouncy when I jump up and down?** If the floors are bouncy, that could mean the joists are overspanned. On the other hand, this could be normal. Bouncy floors are called deflecting floors and there are many perfectly strong and code-built floor systems that can result in bouncy floors. Be sure to alert your home inspector to bouncy floors; an experienced inspector can help you understand if this is normal deflection or an indication of problematic overspanning.

6. **Are the walls plumb? Or are they tilting out?** Sight the walls of the house. Walls that tilt can indicate significant structural

problems. Look especially at structural pony walls, or short walls, in basements and attics.

7. **Are the floors squeaky?** This is usually not a structural concern, but an indication of inadequate adhesive used in the subfloor or inadequate installation of the finish floor. The best time to repair squeaky floors is when replacing finish floor systems—this is when the framing layout can be seen and screws can be used to secure loose subfloor.

OVERSPANNING

One common framing problem is overspanning. This is when a structural support such as a floor joist is run too long without support. This could cause the structure to sag and deflect excessively. To prevent this, engineers and contractors use span tables to determine the proper size of lumber to use for a given span. A large span of 16 feet may require a 2 × 12 floor joist, where a small span of 4 feet may just need a 2 × 4.

These 2 × 4 roof rafters are overspanned and sagging.

SPANNING

Rule of Thumb: I like to use this joist spans rule when looking at framing to see if it is overspanned. This is *not* a substitute for proper engineering but I use it as a finger-to-the-wind guideline for estimating floor joist and roof rafter spans.

- **Floor Joists:** dimension of lumber multiplied by 1.5 equals the maximum allowed span when installed at 16 inches on center. This means a 2 × 8 floor joist should be able to span roughly 12 feet.
- **Roof Rafters:** Dimension of lumber multiplied by two equals the maximum allowed span when installed at 16 inches OC (on center). This means a 2 × 6 roof rafter should be able to span roughly 12 feet.

ACCESS

Few people think of the quality of the access above or below their house as a core system, but houses with marginal access below the house or into the attic have a serious drawback, especially if they are old: how will you make repairs if you have an inaccessible crawl space or no attic space at all? Poor access can be characteristic of cabin-like construction, and in older homes it can make projects unpleasant, expensive, and often unbearable. A lot of new houses have this problem too—think of townhouses and condominiums with no attic or below-floor space for access. When the building is new, one hopes that this will not be an issue for a long time—hard to tell how long, but hopefully 50 years or more. Some large, grand houses have access problems: think large steep roofs with masonry chimneys that require scaffolding to access. Whether big or small, cabin or mansion, limited access can make updates and repairs expensive.

Poor Access: Slab on Grade and Flat Roof

A great example of a house that was doomed by poor access is a neat mid-century house I inspected that had a slab on grade foundation and a flat roof. The home was built in the 1950s. Its in-floor radiant heating system had failed and the house needed new wiring and new plumbing. It was a neat house, but implementing these updates was going to be challenging as there was no place to run these new systems. I suggested installing a pitched roof with an attic space but this would be very expensive. Bottom line: limited access made updating this old house complex and expensive.

TIGHT CRAWL SPACE BELOW THE HOUSE

Even homes that have crawl spaces can be miserable to own if the crawl space is extremely difficult to access. How can you inspect it? How can you repair it? For houses with a tight crawl space, I often recommend additional excavation, which can be expensive and should be done by a qualified general contractor to avoid undermining the footings.

MARGINAL LOT ACCESS

Houses with poor access to the house, such as steep dirt driveways, will have limited resale appeal. Such a house might work for you if you are of the thrill-seeking variety; but when it comes time to sell the house, the pool of potential buyers will be small if merely driving to the house proves to be an adventure. Marginal access to the house will also add cost whenever you repair the house. A common style of urban house that often sells for less is the "walk up," where one has to walk up a flight of stairs to access the house. The good news on houses like this is they are often less expensive as a concession for their marginal access. Again, *every house is a great house for the right person at the right price!*

The only way to get from the garage at the top of the hill to the house is on this long metal gangplank.

FLOOR PLAN

It seems as if everybody loves coming into a house and changing the floor plan. "Is this a load-bearing wall?" is one of the most common questions I am asked. The question is usually followed by a grand vision of how they will transform the house by removing a few walls.

In reality, it's often a good idea, especially when removing a wall, which could open up the kitchen, dining room, and living room space. However, knocking out walls and moving walls around is usually complex and is not something you do casually. It is the type of project that often gets done as part of a larger renovation and costs can quickly mount as questions and obstacles arise: how do you repair the floor and ceiling and wall finishes? What if there is plumbing or wiring in the wall? Projects like this are often more complex than one imagines at the outset, emphasizing why the floor plan is at the core of what you are buying.

If you think it's not such a big deal to remove a wall in a kitchen during a renovation, try having bedrooms on the wrong floor, the stairs in the wrong place, or the living room on the dark side of the house.

The impact of a dysfunctional floor plan is the bane of every architect and can be expensive to correct. Minor tweaks in the floor plan are often easily achievable and can have great benefits at low costs. But significant changes to the floor plan may not be cost-effective. Remember, dysfunctional floor plans can be indicative of dysfunctional houses or at least a house that is not well suited to your needs.

This can be subjective, but take your time and think about how this house will work for your life.

- Is this floor plan best suited for a couple but you have a young family?
- Is this a family house and you want to downsize?
- If you have a baby, will this house not allow for growth, resulting in you needing to buy a new house?

You get the idea. The best real estate professionals and architects are good at thinking about floor plans and you should reach out for this professional expertise.

STAIR QUALITY AND LOCATIONS

Stairs are difficult to build and difficult to move. They also take up a lot of square footage inside your home. Think about this if you want to add a second floor to your house. Let's say your second floor addition adds 400 square feet to your house. You are likely to lose around 40 square feet building a stair system to get you there. This can reduce the overall benefit of going up,

especially if that 40 feet disrupts your existing floor plan. In addition, old homes with steep and unsafe stairs can be nearly impossible to correct in a cost-effective way. Homes with unsafe stairs to the second floor and low ceiling height on the second floor have square footage that is not as valuable; this downside can be difficult and simply not cost-effective to repair or improve.

KITCHEN SPACE

In the kitchen, be sure the home has the space you need for your family: Look at both the counter top space and the pantry space. The visible parts of the kitchen are cosmetic and can be very expensive to change, but in my mind they are not the bones of the house; kitchen finishes are a disposable system. Remember that the next time you spend $50,000 on high-end kitchen finishes.

Kitchens generally have service lives of 15 to 35 years. After which some amount of updating is usually needed. New kitchens can add comfort and value to a home, but the bones of a kitchen are what you really need to focus on. Having to add additional space for a kitchen can get expensive, especially if you are bumping out the back of the house.

CORE SYSTEMS SUMMARY

This completes our overview of core systems. Remember, this book does not have to be read from cover to cover like a novel; I encourage you to go back to these two critical chapters and review what we have gone over. The more you pick this book up and review these points, the more comfortable you will become with them and the more fun you will have looking at houses.

ENTRENCHED SYSTEMS I **6**
SIDING AND CHIMNEYS

Systems that periodically need updating, but are complex to update and more expensive to update are "entrenched systems." These are systems that are more difficult to determine the scope of the repair, adding uncertainty about the final costs to repair, replace, or update.

The most pervasive entrenched system that can cause headache and financial pain for homebuyers and homeowners is the siding system.

SIDING SYSTEMS

Siding falls into the category of an entrenched system. It is a system that is replaceable, but the system is expensive and complex. Some siding systems, if installed properly, can last for the life of the structure. Other siding systems have been known to fail catastrophically in less than 10 years.

Siding systems are installed to protect the home from the elements of the outdoor environment and they are subject to constant degradation from ultraviolet radiation, wind, and water. A siding system must work in conjunction with a weather resistive barrier installed below the siding as well as integration into windows, doors, decks, and rooflines.

This chapter will give you critical background to understand many of the most commonly installed siding systems as well as the flashings and weather barriers that are the key to their success or failure. You will also learn strategies for looking at siding to see for yourself if expensive repairs could be needed and you will learn how the overall house design creates risky or reliable siding systems.

Guiding Principle

The most common location of siding failure is where one system stops and another starts: for example, roof to wall junctures or siding to window junctures or where a chimney goes through a roof. At junctures like these, flashings are used to prevent water leakage.

THE EXTERIOR ENVELOPE

The exterior envelope is an important term to understand when thinking about the outsides of buildings. This is a catch-all term that includes how siding integrates with roofs, decks, windows, and doors—the "skin" of the building. Some traditional house designs with simple rooflines and large roof overhangs don't have what I would consider an envelope; the systems can be easily distinguished: siding, windows, roofs, deck. Other house designs can be more complicated with flat roofs, exposed siding, and rooftop decks; these buildings have an envelope where it is difficult to distinguish where siding stops and windows and roofs begin.

Compare this home with the one on the following page. Notice how this old house has exterior features that are distinguishable, but the modern house on the next page has windows, decks, siding, and a roof that all connect together, making it more complex.

FLASHINGS

Flashings are generally bent pieces of metal that span the gap left by a penetration into a roof or siding system. For example, a window will have a head flashing on top of the window that will prevent water from getting behind the siding where the window has been cut in—the metal will go under the siding and over the window. The nuance of flashing detail can get confusing—leave this to your home inspector. But when you are out

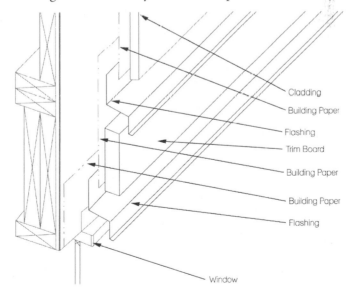

Cladding

Building Paper

Flashing

Trim Board

Building Paper

Building Paper

Flashing

Window

looking at homes, look at where the siding starts, stops, and changes direction. You don't need to be an expert to see if the details around these siding penetrations look professional and clean or sloppy and inconsistent.

The flashing here does not shed water and has rotted over time because the base of these shingles has been sitting in water.

Tip: Look to see if flashing details and exterior trim are properly sloped to drain. Flashings or trim with reverse slope or even a flat aspect can cause water to drain into the envelope causing water problems.

Tip: Most people are surprised to learn that most siding leaks. The weather resistive barrier installed below the siding is the key to keeping the building dry and performing as intended.

WEATHER RESISTIVE BARRIERS

The primary purpose of the weather resistive barrier (WRB) is to keep the building materials dry that are below the siding. This is more complex than you might imagine as you must stop water from penetrating from the outside while also allowing vapor to escape from the inside—thus the ideal WRB is a breathable barrier. WRBs come in two primary forms: the old building paper or tar paper and more modern housewraps such as the commonly installed Tyvek made by DuPont Corporation.

The performance of the WRB can make all the difference to a siding system. Unfortunately, there are a lot of variables with WRBs and they are not visible to inspection once the siding goes on, so it can be nearly impossible to determine if the WRBs are installed at all or performing correctly.

Variables in WRBs include proper installation techniques and selection of the correct WRB for the siding system and local climate conditions—for example, builders in Mississippi may use a different WRB than builders in Nevada.

There is not much you can look for with WRBs since they are not visible. However, understanding the concept of WRBs is important context for understanding how siding systems work. The topic of WRBs is confusing and there are no simple "correct choices" that can apply to every siding system in every part of the country. Educated homebuyers will understand the importance of WRBs should they come up during inspection or later repair work.

EXPOSURE AND SIDING

The amount you worry about your siding should be in direct pro-

Thw side of this house was getting especially wet during a rainstorm.

portion to the amount your building is exposed to the weather. For example, one-story buildings with generous roof overhangs rarely have extensive siding problems, while three-story buildings with no roof overhangs and lots of exposure to the weather are likely to have problems.

Rule of Thumb: The nicer the view from inside the home, and the more light that is coming into the home, the more I would worry about the exterior envelope.

The southeast-facing turret is going to take a lot of weather.

Siding Red Flags to Look For

It's pretty easy to spot shoddy workmanship on an exterior. Look for loose and poorly installed siding.

Be sure to look most closely on the sides of the house that are exposed to the weather.

Left: Sloppy flashing detail—notice how the flashing is incomplete and doesn't extend to the corner. Right: Loose and poorly fastened siding.

SOME SIDING BASICS

From a building science perspective, there are three basic types of siding systems: Barrier systems, reservoir siding systems, and drainage plane systems.

1. **A barrier system** is designed to build a water-resistive barrier between the house and the outdoor elements. The siding material is installed directly on top of a weather resistive barrier. Examples are lap siding, shingle siding, board and batten siding, plywood siding, fiber-cement  siding, and synthetic stucco siding. Most siding systems are barrier systems. The drawback to this type of system is if water gets behind a barrier system, it may become trapped, which should always be avoided. *Remember, buildings that get wet DO NOT rot; buildings that stay wet WILL rot.*

2. **A reservoir siding system** will soak up water when it gets wet. These are masonry assemblies, such as brick and stucco when installed on wood-framed houses. When these systems dry, they dry in two directions: to the outside and to the inside. This is because moisture travels from a higher concentration to a lower concentration.

Brick is a classic reservoir siding system. The key to a reservoir siding system is for air to get behind the siding, allowing it to dry. If a wall assembly has a well executed weather barrier and good dry potential, a reservoir siding system can last 100 years or more.

3. **A drainage plane system** is similar to a reservoir siding system

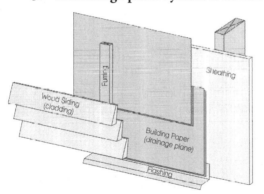

in that it allows air to move behind the siding to create dry potential. The difference is that some of these systems are done using materials that do not necessarily store water—such as brick. You may see modern fiber-cement siding installed on wood batten strips so that air can move behind the siding. This is a newer siding system often found on new townhouses and condominiums. Another name for these systems is a rainscreen system.

The rainscreen system allows air to move behind the siding, providing dry potential.

TYPES OF SIDING

There are a lot of different ways to side a building. In this section we'll go over some of the most common types of siding systems. Let's start by looking at the different types of wood siding.

The most common forms of wood siding are shingles, lap siding (sometimes called clapboard), tongue and groove, shiplap, board and batten, and plywood.

Wood siding is almost always installed as a barrier siding system. This is an old and accepted way to side a house. Where the siding is well installed and done in old growth lumber and on a house without too much exposure, wood siding systems can last over 100 years.

Modern wood siding is a quality product, but it is generally inferior to its old-growth predecessor; new-growth wood has less hardwood and more sapwood. That makes new-growth wood more vulnerable to cupping, splitting, and wood decay, especially when exposed to the weather. Modern wood siding can fail in as few as 25 years, fewer still if a poor quality product is installed poorly on an exposed building.

WOOD QUALITY

The types of wood most often used for exterior siding work are woods with natural resistance to decay such as cedar and redwood. These woods have tannic acid in the wood that helps them resist wood fungal rot.

The quality of wood siding can vary significantly. The best quality wood is often called #1 or clear. Cedar shingles, for example, are often sold as #1s or #2s to indicate the quality of the wood. Beveled cedar siding can be "clear," without knots, or "tight knot," with knots. Generally, clear wood is more expensive and of higher quality; it will last longer and be more dimensionally stable.

In the Pacific Northwest, you might find wood siding as old as 100 years on some buildings. Many mid-century homes have incredibly thick wood siding that can last for the life of the building. You might find quality "combed cedar" shingle siding on homes from the 1950s and beautiful tongue and groove clear cedar on homes from the 1970s—all in good condition, especially if well protected. Wood siding from the 1980s and more recent tends to be of generally lower quality though there are exceptions. Cedar shingles still seem to be an excellent quality wood siding choice. Board and batten siding is common on houses built where people felled their own lumber from local trees on the property. Thick slabs of hand-milled cedar are nailed on with wood batten strips covering the gaps.

The type of wood siding used in a community will follow patterns that will be regional and age specific. What was the wood being harvested near your community and when were they harvesting this wood? The answer to this question may influence the quality of the wood siding installed on the houses in your community. In the Southeast, it could be cypress; in Northern California, redwood; in the Pacific Northwest, cedar.

Look for the trends you see in your home searches. It can be fun to identify products you like the look of in your region and then learn more about them—such as how long they last and what types of maintenance can be expected.

Note: A common wood siding material used in modern homes is "primed spruce" trim. This is inferior to cedar because it has no natural resistance to decay. I often see houses just a few years old with a few rotting bits of spruce trim.

What to Look for in Failing Siding

- Peeling and failing paint—paint jobs are expensive, but should be routine maintenance

- Faded stain and discolored shingles
- Wood rot and decay

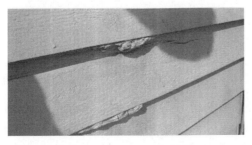

Red flag: Mushrooms growing out of siding.

- Knots that have fallen out of the siding
- Cupping and splitting siding

- Wood decay in spruce trim

Where to Look for Failing Siding

- Weather-exposed aspects of the building—often the southwest corner
- Roof/wall junctures
- Deck/wall junctures
- Around windows—especially sills
- Below atrium skylights
- Near the ground and at the base of downspouts

FREQUENTLY ASKED QUESTIONS

Q: I have noticed that some older houses with wood lap siding seem to have chronic problems with the paint job bubbling and falling off in great flakes. Why?

A. This could be from a poorly prepared paint job, but there is a good chance that this was caused by air moving through the house from the inside to the outside. Remember, moisture goes from concentrations of

more to less. Moisture can move through your walls as the building dries to the exterior. If the siding is covered in latex paint, the siding cannot breathe and the moisture is trapped. The resulting moisture below the paint causes the paint to bubble or blister and separate from the wood siding.

Q: What is the difference between stain and paint?

A: Paint is a thick coating that can be measured in millimeters of build-up. Stain is a penetrating liquid that soaks into the wood rather than coating it. Generally, paint jobs can last longer but require high replacement costs due to all the preparation of scraping off the failing paint. Stain is a much easier reapplication because you don't have flaking paint to deal with.

PLYWOOD SIDING AND SINGLE WALLS SYSTEMS

Most everyone is familiar with plywood. It is manufactured by taking trees and running them through a lathe to remove a thin sheet of wood from the tree as it spins around, like a roll of paper towels. These thin sheets are then glued together to form a panel. The result is a durable building material that stands up to water better than its Oriented Strand Board (OSB) cousin. OSB comes in sheets like plywood but it looks like chips of wood glued together rather than sheets of veneer glued together. Because OSB is made from chips, the cell structure in the wood has been more heavily damaged in manufacturing—thus the OSB is more susceptible than plywood to wood decay, mold, and fungus.

Plywood siding was used a lot in the 1970s into the 1980s. Look for areas of delamination, especially on weather-exposed sides of the building and near the ground. Many homes with plywood siding are installed as "single wall systems." These types of homes use the plywood for *both* the sheathing and the siding. This is different from a conventional double wall siding system where you have sheathing, a weather resistive barrier, and then a siding product. Generally, single wall buildings are less durable and more vulnerable to water problems.

Tip: If you are buying a house that is single wall construction, you can add another layer of siding over the top of the plywood. This is often done in conjunction with window updating and can be an excellent though expensive repair/upgrade.

HARDBOARD SIDING—OSB AND OTHERS

The term hardboard describes siding products made from a composite of wood rather than solid wood—think chips of wood glued together. Various forms of hardboard siding have been around for over 100 years, though these older versions are not widely installed. Some of these older products are surprisingly reliable—I have seen some hardboards do well from the 1970s. However, most of the hardboard siding systems you are likely to encounter were manufactured around the 1990s.

The 1990s ushered in a slew of new composite wood siding products, all of which could somewhat accurately be referred to as hardboard siding.[1]

Unfortunately, virtually every company that made hardboard siding in the 1990s has been involved in class-action lawsuits due to the premature failure of their siding.

Examples Include

- Louisiana Pacific (LP)
- Inner-Seal siding (OSB)
- Weyerhaeuser
- Masonite (Omniwood)
- Masonite (Hardboard)
- Forestex
- ABTCO

The hole in this siding was made from a nail head that has been sucked through the swelling and failing siding.

If you have one of these products on your house or a prospective house, expect the siding to be in some stage of failure where exposed to the weather. Parts of the building protected from the weather may be fine, including up under eaves and on the home's north side.

Unfortunately, most or all of the class action lawsuits have been settled so there is generally no money available now to replace failed siding.

---

1. Technically OSB siding is not a hardboard siding but we will lump it here to make things a bit more simple.

Replacing siding can be expensive—a complex project to an entrenched system.

Hardboard sidings are installed prior to drainage plane systems. Expect these to be installed as barrier systems.

What to Look for on Hardboard Siding Systems

- Delaminating of the bottom lip of the lap siding
- Swelling around nail heads, cuts, and penetrations through the siding
- Water damage around windows where the siding has been cut
- Water damage by decks or below roof/wall junctures or near the ground where the siding may be getting wet
- Mushrooms growing out of the siding
- Wavy bowed areas of siding

FIBER CEMENT SIDING

For the most part, these modern fiber-cement siding systems appear to be a huge improvement over the hardboard siding products they replaced. Fiber cement is dimensionally stable, which means it resists cupping and warping and it can hold paint well (I have seen paint jobs last for over 12 years on fiber-cement). Modern fiber-cement is roughly 98 percent cement with a small amount of wood fiber used to bond the cement together. Modern fiber-cement comes in lap siding, panels of siding meant to look like shingles, and sheets of siding like plywood. Fiber-cement siding can be found installed as a drainage plane system or a barrier system.

This product started being widely installed in the early 2000s and generally performs well. Like all siding products, fiber-cement siding must be properly installed.

You can generally identify a fiber-cement siding by rapping on it—it will sound hard like cement.

ASBESTOS CEMENT SIDING

The old cement siding systems used asbestos fibers to bond the cement together. These are quality siding systems usually installed as tiles. Expect to see a few damaged tiles or repairs done using caulking and adhesives. These tiles are very brittle so they are subject to physical damage. The first asbestos cement tile systems were often installed like vinyl siding: over the top of another siding system.

If you want to replace this siding, expect a disposal liability for the asbestos content. As the siding is on the outside of the house, it should not pose a signifi-cant indoor air quality risk, especially if kept well painted.

These shingles were most likely installed as barrier systems and may have another layer of siding underneath.

What to Look For

- Cracked and damaged tiles

BRICK

When you are looking at a brick house, remember that you are most likely looking at a wood framed house with a veneer of brick over the top that is acting as a siding system. If you see brick inside and outside, then you may be looking at a structure literally built of brick; think commercial loft spaces.

Brick is one of my favorite siding systems. It is a classic reservoir siding system; this means you should see weep holes at the base of the brick and there should be an unseen air gap between the back of the brick and the sheathing of the house. (See first diagram on page 81.)

Brick can be expensive to repair and some people get the sense that this makes it bad siding. Keep in mind that I sometimes see brick siding that is 80 years old and hardly any maintenance has been done to it in all that time. Find another siding product like that! However, if no mainte-nance has been done for years, expect the need for some repairs.

What to Look For

- Check where the brick spans over windows and doors. These areas usually have a stone or a metal lintel.[2] Do these appear to be in good shape?

---

2. A lintel is a structural horizontal member that spans an opening between two vertical supports.

- Check the mortar between the brick. Is it old and falling apart? Do the bricks stick out like teeth in a receding gumline?
- Sight along the walls of the house. Be sure the brick is not bowing. Structural problems with brick can be expensive to repair.
- Look for stair-step cracks in the brick that indicate structural movement in the brick wall and/or the house.

Stair-step cracks and a steel lintel.

Vocabulary

Tuck Pointing: Repairs to brick mortar involve removing the old mortar between the bricks and applying new mortar. This repair is often called "tuck pointing" the brick.

Weep Holes: Look for "weep holes," at the base of brick siding. Brick siding needs to breathe because it is a reservoir siding system. The weep holes at the base of the siding are intentional—they allow air to move behind the brick creating dry potential. People often fill these weep holes thinking the masons missed a spot. They did not! Do not do this! Weep holes are important. (See image on page 80.)

The Trick with Brick

People often notice that the old mortar between bricks is sandy and soft. They think that this is an indication of poor workmanship. In fact, it is not. Good masons will try to build a masonry assembly of similar hardness and pour size. Soft bricks should have soft mortar and hard bricks should have hard mortar. An amateur mistake is using hard mortar on soft brick as a repair. This can cause the bricks to spall and fall apart.

ALUMINUM AND VINYL

Both aluminum and vinyl siding are installed as barrier systems. One downside of these siding systems is the way they inhibit a view of the bones of the house; it's much harder, for example, to sight your eyes along the siding to look for settlement or moisture problems because the house has this floating screen over the top.

Aluminum and vinyl siding both need to have proper channel flashings installed around windows and doors and other siding penetrations—often called j-channel flashings. Think of these as proper transitions at penetrations that allow the siding to slide into a channel next to a window or door for a waterproof detail. Installations that are older and have not been carefully detailed will often have poor transitions at siding penetrations. You might even see updated windows in old vinyl siding and the windows are just kind of smeared with caulking around the edges—a sign of an amateur installation.

Aluminum siding was commonly installed in the 1950s through the 1960s and seemed to trail off sometime in the 1970s. Aluminum is a good siding material because it does not rust or rot—it comes prefinished and does not require painting. It does get beat up over time and you may see older aluminum siding with dents and physical damage. I often see old aluminum siding that has been painted because the original powder coating faded. This can work, but it does defeat the original purpose of this siding system—to avoid painting the house.

Vinyl siding is similar to aluminum in many respects but it is made from plastic. Vinyl expands and contracts, so expect to find a few panels that have slid out of position. Vinyl is a lightweight material and can be vulnerable to wind damage. Over time, the vinyl breaks down with UV exposure and the color fades and the material becomes brittle. While you can paint vinyl, this is often a red flag that the siding is old and at the end of its life. Vinyl tends to last roughly 30 years though a lot depends on your willingness to maintain a system that likely does not look so great after being out in the weather for more than 30 years.

What to Look For

- Loose siding panels
- Physically damaged and dented siding—you may even see places where the siding has melted from UV exposure or a nearby grill

- Poor details around windows and penetrations in the siding and missing j-channel flashings

TRADITIONAL STUCCO

Traditional stucco is an ancient building material that was historically applied over masonry buildings. Modern stucco is basically made from Portland cement, lime, and sand and is often installed over wood-framed buildings in the United States and Canada. Quality stucco systems are three or more coats of stucco applied over a lath system, like chicken wire,

that has been mechanically fastened to the side of the house. There are also less expensive systems: two-coat stucco and even one-coat stucco. I like to feel the bottom edge of the stucco to distinguish its quality: Stucco that is built-up less than ⅝ of an inch may be a lower quality one-coat or two-coat installation.

This is a thick, hard coat stucco system—¾ of an inch thick.

Stucco is designed to never need painting. You may want to paint it because you do not like the color of the original tinted finish coat or the original finish is now faded and in poor condition. However, paint can fill the pores of the cement and inhibit the ability of the stucco to breathe and dry. This could conceivably trap water in the stucco and facilitate decay and water damage. Stucco contractors generally do not recommend painting stucco.

The key to making a stucco system perform well is to have the weather resistive barrier below the stucco installed carefully and to have penetrations through the stucco flashed correctly—think windows, decks, roof, and door transitions. The flashings are visible to inspection and can be a telling clue as to the quality of the installation. Unfortunately, during a visual inspection, the weather resistive barrier is not visible. So how can you tell if the stucco is failing? You often *cannot*; the stucco could conceal hidden water damage.

Stucco Red Flags to Look For

- Cracks in stucco, especially around windows and doors
- Water staining on stucco, especially around penetrations
- Thin stucco, which may indicate a lower quality installation

- Damaged metal control joints or flashings

- Bowing or buckling sections of stucco

Stucco Overview

If installed well, stucco is one of the highest quality siding systems. However, experts consider stucco to be a high-risk exterior siding system, especially if the home is not well protected by roof overhangs. Poorly installed stucco can leak and conceal hidden water damage that can be very expensive to repair. Ask your home inspector if they have experience looking at stucco. Look for red flags on your own, but use the experience of your local home inspector and consider hiring a specialist. Specialists can use special moisture probes to look for hidden water damage in stucco systems. They are also especially good at spotting small installation details that many home inspectors miss. Specialists generally come in two types: stucco installers and exterior envelope engineers.

Left: Obvious red flags in a patched stucco system. Right: Quality stucco details around a window.

SYNTHETIC STUCCO

Synthetic stucco is often called EIFS, or Exterior Insulated Finish System. This is essentially foam insulation that has been glued onto the building with a coating of Portland cement stucco over the top. This system will look exactly like stucco, but ironically it could not be more different from a performance standpoint. You may also hear of synthetic stucco as Dryvit, or other brand names.

Synthetic stucco is a barrier system. This means it is designed to keep water out. If water does get behind this system, it has been known to trap water very well. This can cause extensive structural damage to wood buildings in a short period of time and this damage is often not discoverable during a visual inspection. When I am inspecting a house sided with EIFS, I am definitely afraid about what I do not know.

Be cautious of homes with EIFS. I have heard that some home insurance companies will specifically exclude EIFS from their homeowner's coverage. If I were buying a home sided with EIFS, I would consider hiring a contractor who specializes in evaluating EIFS siding. Such a specialist will sometimes use long moisture meter probes to determine if moisture is getting trapped behind the stucco. This is called "destructive testing" and you will need to get permission from the seller before you employ this diagnostic strategy. This will add expense and time to your inspections, but even if they discover that the system is working well, this will be valuable information that can be used again when it comes time to sell.

- You can tell synthetic stucco because when you rap your knuckles on it, it will not sound like cement; it will sound like you are hitting Styrofoam.
- The scary thing with EIFS is that it is hard to tell if it is trapping water. This may not be visible during a visual inspection and is why you may need a specialist.

SIDING CONCLUSION

Siding systems are very expensive and if they need to be updated or even maintained with an expensive paint job, this is something you may be able to spot on your own when you are out looking at houses. Some siding problems can be hard to spot, especially with stucco and synthetic stucco systems—a great reason to hire a good home inspector. Other siding problems are easy to spot; just take the time to look.

Houses with low-maintenance siding systems are much more likely to be low-maintenance houses. It will pay dividends to review this chapter and understand the rudiments of siding systems and envelope designs that are common in your area. If you are looking for a low-maintenance house, try to find a house with a roof design that helps protect the siding and the rest of the building. If you want the look and feel of a more exposed building, be sure to check the siding system and exterior envelope carefully.

CHIMNEYS

Chimneys are a ubiquitous feature in older homes and they are often built into the house or siding, making them entrenched into the home. Chimneys you might be looking at today come in three basic types:

1. Masonry chimneys—usually stone, brick, or block
2. Exposed metal chimneys—often for wood stoves
3. Metal flue liners inside wood chimney chases—visualize a wood box that is sided and wraps around a metal flue pipe.

Basic Chimney History

Masonry chimneys were generally the only type of chimney installed until the 1960s, when the less expensive wood chimney chases began to replace the more expensive masonry chimneys. *One neat trick when looking at homes built in the 1980s to 1990s is that if the house has a masonry chimney, it was probably a more expensive, higher-end house.*

Houses built since the 2000s are unlikely to even have a chimney. This is because modern energy codes eliminated chimneys for energy efficiency reasons. The traditional fireplace is very good at sucking the heat out of your building via the flue with something called the stack effect. Modern houses have replaced the old wood fireplace with direct vent gas log fireplaces and central heating systems.

MASONRY CHIMNEYS

The oldest chimney systems can be pretty humble. These older chimneys are often unlined, meaning a look inside reveals brick or stone, which is not as reliable a surface for venting products of combustion. Starting around the mid-century, masonry chimneys generally became better constructed, often having terra-cotta flue liners. You may see liners as early as the 1900s—this will depend on regional chimney construction trends.

With masonry chimneys, take a moment to think about how much they weigh. Masonry chimneys weigh so much that they typically have their own foundations. So think of your chimney as a second foundation next to your house foundation. It is not uncommon to see the chimney settling relative to the house or the house settling relative to the chimney. Look for floors sloping either down toward the chimney or up away from the chimney. Floors sloping toward the chimney mean the chimney is taking the floors down. Floors sloped away from the chimney indicate

Old river rock chimney—the stones may have come from the beach below.

the house is settling relative to the chimney. This can be a red flag that an expensive structure repair may be needed.

When it comes to looking at houses, you don't need to know everything about chimneys, but you do need to know that it is common to need to make repairs to masonry chimneys and repairs can be simple and inexpensive or complex and expensive, depending on what is wrong.

What to Look for with Masonry Chimneys

- Leaning or twisted chimneys—sight your eyes along the chimney—leaning or twisting could indicate a structural problem with the chimney—think expensive.
- Failing mortar and spalling brick—look for damaged mortar between the brick or damaged brick, especially above the roofline and in basements. This can indicate the need for chimney repairs. Minor failing mortar is pretty typical and not usually too expensive to repair. Extensive damage to brick or failing mortar can get more expensive to repair.

Note: In many cases today, chimneys that require repair simply get removed as the cost to repair them exceeds their value.

Water damage, damaged mortar, and spalling brick—repairs to this chimney can get expensive.

WOOD CHIMNEY CHASES

Wood chimney chases are essentially wood boxes that stick up into the sky. They take much more weather than the rest of the house, so siding failure and water problems will happen with more frequency on these exposed boxes.

What to Look for with Wood Chimneys

- Wood decay
- Water stains
- Rot

ENTRENCHED SYSTEMS II **7**
IN THE WALLS

In addition to siding, there are more entrenched systems that you should understand in a cursory way to better prepare yourself for looking at and understanding houses. These include branch wiring, heating and cooling distribution systems, water piping systems, windows, insulation (both in walls and in vaulted ceilings), and ventilation.

Entrenched Systems Review

- Periodically in need of updating, but are more complex to update and often more expensive.
- Often more difficult to determine where repairs begin and end and can be more difficult to estimate repair and updating costs.

In this chapter, we learn about systems that are often behind the walls and connected into the house—systems where replacement and updating is complex due to limited access and visibility.

Let's take a look at each system.

BRANCH WIRING

The electrical system is a critical component to the home for both your comfort and safety. For the purposes of learning to look at homes, you really don't have to know the finer points of the electrical code. You simply need to understand electrical system basics. Your home inspector and electrician can handle the more complex issues.

Keeping it Simple

I like to break down the electrical system into three parts:

1. Service equipment—your electric meter, panel, and wires coming to the house from the utility
2. Branch wiring—all the wire running around your house
3. Finish wiring—the lights, switches, and receptacles

Because the finishes of your walls, ceilings, and floors are obstructing access to most of the wires in the house, the branch wiring system is difficult to update and is an entrenched system. Rewiring your house could require opening up walls and other finishes. The alternative is fishing wire through cavities of the house. Both of these approaches are time-consuming and labor-intensive—which means expensive. By contrast, repairs to the electrical service equipment and finish wiring are less complex because they are easy to access. Thus, reliable estimates for repairs and updates are easier to obtain. Again, the guiding principle is to be cautious about what we *do not* know—like wiring behind walls.

Tip: Unfinished basements, crawl spaces, and easily accessible attics can be very helpful when rewiring because you have access for running new wire.

AMATEUR WIRING

One of the most basic things we don't want to see is amateur workmanship of the wiring system. This can mean hidden surprises behind finishes. Believe it or not, you don't need to be an electrician to spot amateur or incomplete wiring.

What to Look For
- Wiring cable loosely run and exposed
- Open splices and wire nuts—you should never really see wire nuts
- Open junction boxes and missing cover plates (pictured below)

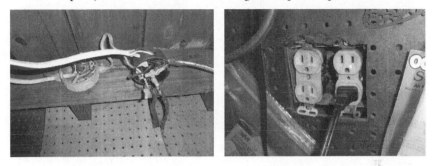

- Correctly wired outlets. You can test this (in an amateur way) using an inexpensive circuit tester that you can purchase at your hardware store
- "False grounds." This is when an old two-wire circuit has a modern three-prong receptacle installed. Just because you see three-prong receptacles in an old house does not mean it is a modern three-wire system. It could be missing the ground wire—indicating older two-wire wiring. Your circuit tester can tell you this.

WIRING IN OLDER HOMES

If you have ever looked at buying an older home, your real estate agent or your friends have probably cautioned you that the wiring could be unsafe. Why? The simple answer is old homes don't have much wire in them.

For example, compare a 1920s house to a new house, both the same size with original wiring. Why is the older house less safe? Less wire means more chances of overloading and that means more chances for overheating—think lots of extension cords and power strips drawing more and more

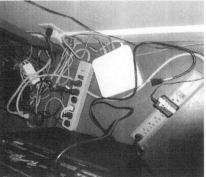

Modern Families Need Modern Wiring

Moving a modern family into an old house with original wiring is like driving a Model T Ford on the Autobahn. The wiring in an old house was simply never designed to handle all the loads and expectations we have for wiring today. Put yourself in 1920 and ask, "What do I own that I need to plug in?" The answer: Not much. Now think about all the gadgets and gizmos you plug in today in your kitchen, your office, your bathroom, and load all that stuff onto a 100-year-old wire. That's a recipe for a fire.

loads from just a few old wires, on which insulation could be wearing thin in places and connections could be coming loose.

KNOB-AND-TUBE WIRING

This is the original soldered wiring system where wires are run through ceramic knobs and tubes. These wires are not contained inside a non-metallic sheathed cable, as we would do today. You can expect to see knob-and-tube wiring in homes from the late 1880s to mid-1950s. Many insurance companies will not insure your house if you have knob-and-tube wiring, so be sure to ask your insurance company.

Knob-and-tube wiring does not marry well with modern wiring and it should never be buried in insulation. Inspectors will only be able to see wire where it is exposed, so it is hard to know how much knob and tube an old house may have. It is common for even well updated older homes to still employ several knob-and-tube circuits. However, you do not want the combination of this older wiring and an under-wired house since it can

Typical amateur splice of modern wiring on old knob-and-tube wiring. This is unsafe.

lead to overloading. This is a safety hazard. If you are extensively renovating an old house, plan on updating all of this old wiring where it is uncovered; this is your opportunity to update an old entrenched system.

ALUMINUM SINGLE-STRAND WIRING

This wiring was installed from roughly 1965 to 1975 due to shortages of copper. The problem is when it is used for 15 and 20 amp circuits, it is a known fire hazard. One study shows that homes wired before 1972 with single-strand aluminum wire are 55 times more likely to have one or more wire connections at outlets reaching fire hazard conditions for two primary reasons:

> ### Multi-Strand Aluminum Wire
>
> Multi-strand aluminum wire, where multiple thin strands are bundled together to create a large conductor, is a wire that we still use all the time today. This multi-strand aluminum wire is safe and not a reportable condition.

1. Aluminum wire expands and contracts, causing wiring connections to come loose.
2. Aluminum can fatigue and break down, causing resistance and overheating.

While the "field" of the wire is generally reliable, it may become loose or fatigued where it connects to fixtures—loose or damaged connections cause arcing. Arcing is when an electric current, often strong, brief, and luminous, jumps across a gap—not something you want inside your home.

Repairs can be made to this wire using crimping systems to crimp copper wire onto the aluminum wire. But be wary of this repair if a professional did not complete it. The Consumer Product Safety Commission recommends only three types of repairs for this wire, one of which is complete replacement.[1]

---

1. For more information see www.cpsc.gov//PageFiles/118856/516.pdf.

MODERN WIRING

Modern wiring is done using predominantly sheathed non-metallic (NM) cable. This is a rubber-like sheathing that wraps around three or four wires, depending on the type of circuit that is run. The first generations of NM cable started in the 1950s after knob-and-tube was phased out. First generation NM cable did not have an equipment ground—think two-prong outlet. Starting in the 1960s, an equipment ground was added to create the modern three wire, three-prong type outlet that we are familiar with today.

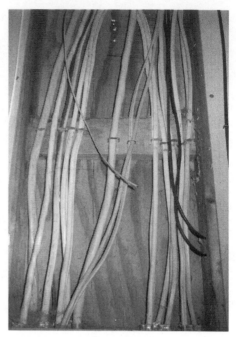

FREQUENTLY ASKED QUESTIONS

Q: In my old house, when I turn on my hair dryer, my circuit breaker trips. Why does this happen?

A: Generally, this type of problem is indicative of an under-wired house. You are trying to pull too much electricity through too small a wire and the breaker trips to protect you. It does not want that wire to work too hard and get hot, which could lead to a fire. This can be a hard thing to verify or test during a home inspection, but if your electric panel has few breakers, the house has few circuits. Thus you should expect this to be a problem. If you are experiencing frequent tripping of a breaker or a GFCI (Ground Fault Circuit Interrupters) breaker, you should have this evaluated by an electrician as soon as possible. There could be an important reason for this, such as a defective breaker.

Q: What is the difference between amperage and voltage?

A: I like to think of electricity in terms of water flow because it helps me visualize these invisible electrons moving. Think of amperage as the diameter of the water pipe and think of voltage as the water pressure. Thin wires can only carry so much amperage, so we protect a small #14 wire with a 15-amp breaker. If you run more than 15 amps through this wire, the breaker should trip to prevent over-heating.

All of our homes in the United States run on essentially the same voltage: 110/220 volts. Most of the stuff in our homes runs on 110: lights, outlets, refrigerators, televisions, and stereos. When you see some of those circuit breakers that have a bridge between them to double them up, these are 220-volt circuits—these ones get double the voltage to make heat for things like hot water, your range, and your clothes dryer.

Q: Why are some breakers in my electric panel connected by a bar or a bridge?

A: If you want to make heat with electricity on purpose, we double up the voltage from 110 to 220 volts. This is what runs electric clothes dryers, cooktops, ovens, heaters, and water heaters—220-volt breakers protect these circuits. The bridge essentially connects two 110 volt circuits, resulting in a single 220 volt circuit.

HEATING AND COOLING DISTRIBUTION

Heating and cooling distribution systems such as ductwork or boiler pipes are often concealed behind walls, ceilings, and floors, making them difficult to access for repairs and updates. Homes that do not have central heating distribution systems can be difficult to retrofit with ducts, as there may be no space to run ducts and running boiler pipes can be expensive. For this reason, these heating and cooling distribution systems are considered an entrenched system in a house.

Many heating distribution systems, if installed well, can last for the life of the building or at least for 100 years.

When comparing homes, it is smart to compare how they are heated and cooled. Often small condominiums employ simple electric heaters and don't have much of a distribution system for heating and cooling. This can be fine for a small space. You may not want such a humble system, however, if you are looking at heating and cooling a 3500-square-foot house.

Below you will find some basic information about the two most common types of central heating and cooling distribution methods.

DUCTWORK

Ductwork is the most common method for moving hot or cold air around a house. Ducts are metal pipes or plastic tubes that often run in your basement, attic, or crawl space and inside wall and floor cavities. As a general rule, you don't want to see your ductwork unless your home has an industrial look. Retrofitting ducts can involve opening up walls and ceilings. This is expensive and often even cost-prohibitive.

Ducts can generally be divided into two parts:

1. **Supply Air:** The conditioned air coming off your central heating or cooling system.
2. **Return Air:** The larger ducts that take unconditioned inside air and return it to your air handler for conditioning.

A Few Ductwork Tips

- **Old House Tip:** Older homes with renovations to the second floor commonly have inadequate or poorly sized ducts running to the second floor.
- **Mid-Century Tip:** Mid-century homes sometimes have a full cold air return system, which is a nice way of doing the ductwork. In this system, you have both a supply and a return in each room. This creates more even heating throughout the house. This design fell out of favor with the building industry because it was less expensive to run a single large cold air return in the middle of the house, which is employed in nearly all homes today. A single large return system is not as efficient at heating a home evenly and can result in problematic pressure differentials inside your home.
- **Efficiency Tip:** Old ductwork leaks lots of air. If your ducts are located in an unconditioned space like the attic or the crawl space, this means they are leaking energy to the outdoors. Consider a tune-up where you air-seal and insulate the ducts to save energy.
- **Inspection Tip:** Check inside ducts. I often see ducts that need to be cleaned and sometimes I will find dead carpenter ants. If a house was distressed and has been spit-shined for a quick flip, extremely dirty ducts sometimes indicate that the house has been abused.

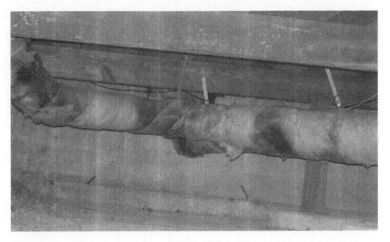

The black stains on the fiberglass insulation of these ducts is dirt from air leakage.

BOILER PIPES

If your heating system is a boiler, expect the need for pipes to move water or steam through the building. These types of heating systems are called boiler systems or sometimes "hydronic" heating systems, which basically means water-based heat delivery.

- Old buildings have metal distribution pipes. If these are galvanized steel pipes, they could be close to the end of their service lives. During a home inspection, the system is run to determine if all of the radiators get hot. But even if they work during inspection, old distribution piping makes me nervous; you should expect these old pipes to need repairs and updates at some point.
- New buildings often use plastic pipes or tubing to move the hot water in a heating system. Some of these tubing systems have had class action lawsuits filed against them. Be especially wary of polybutylene (PB 2110—a gray plastic tubing) or Kitec (an orange plastic tubing) distribution piping.
- Many boiler systems today run hot water through a system of pipes or tubes in the floor of the house. This type of system is referred to as a radiant floor heating system and it has become very popular. Radiant floor systems can be difficult to test during warm weather because the temperature of the heated floor is often not much above the ambient temperature of the floor on a warm summer day. Your inspector may use an infrared imaging

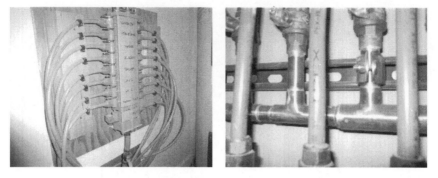

Left: PB 2110 manifold. Right: Orange Kitec.

camera, which can usually "see" the heat from the warm pipes in the floor. Beware of radiant systems that have been retrofit into older homes—these systems are complex and usually executed best when the house was designed for them in the first place.

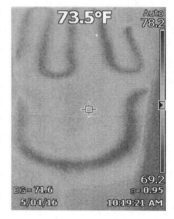

• Open-loop heating systems are a relatively new design where the hot water heating for domestic supply shares the same water as the hot water used to heat your house. Think of it this way: the hot water in your shower could be the same hot water that is in your radiator.

These systems became popular because they are less expensive to install—one appliance does hot water and heating and they can be energy efficient. A drawback to these systems is that new oxygen is constantly being introduced to the system as new water circulates through. This is significantly different from the older closed-loop boiler systems where the same water might circulate through the radiator pipes for years. All this new oxygen can be more corrosive and cause myriad problems to the hydronic heating system. In addition, you run the risk of having stagnant water in the pipes that could cause health safety concerns when this stagnant water from the heating pipes gets flushed into the domestic water piping system. I would be wary of open-loop systems and hire a local specialist to consult with you about options for converting an open-loop system into a closed loop.

WATER SUPPLY PIPES

When touring homes, you need to know something about the types of materials commonly used for home plumbing systems. Piping systems in the home are entrenched systems because they are often concealed and can be more complicated to replace, especially if wall or ceiling finishes need to be opened up. Below you will find some basic information about common types of materials used to distribute water through the house.

Galvanized Steel: This is the classic old house piping. Most homes used this until the 1960s. The drawback with galvanized steel pipe is that the galvanization, which was used to prevent rust, wears off and over time the insides of the pipe occlude with rust (pictured below). Be suspicious of galvanized steel piping. You will need to update this pipe at some point and typically sooner than later. The urgency will depend on functional flow and the overall condition of the pipe. Test multiple faucets at once to ensure enough water is still flowing through the pipes to provide adequate performance.

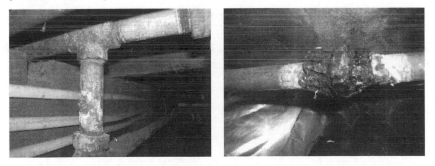

Copper: Copper is my favorite piping system. However, in some parts of the country that have hard water, the copper can break down and develop pits that lead to premature leaks and failure. In areas with soft water, copper has nearly an unlimited useful service life. PEX tubing and CPVC are replacing copper today because copper has become expensive. Copper is a soldered system, meaning the pipes are soldered or sweated together. Some of the older soldering systems contained lead. If you are concerned about water quality, you should take a water sample to a lab for testing.

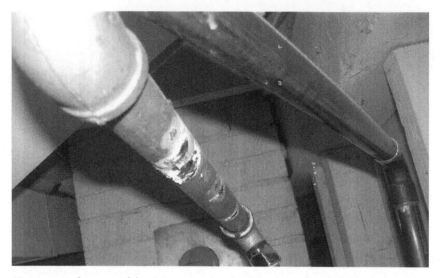

You can see where part of the piping system here has been updated with copper (right) and the remaining steel pipe (left) is failing.

PEX: PEX is a plastic tubing system. The tubing comes in coils and can save a lot of money on labor because in can be uncoiled and run long distances without the need for soldering or gluing pipes together. But with all plastic piping, be wary of installation: This is a durable and quality tubing system, but it is only as good as the quality of the fittings.

CPVC: CPVC is white rigid plastic pipe. The pipe is installed by gluing pipes together using glue and fittings. This pipe is vulnerable to physical damage because it can crack and is easily penetrated by an errant framing nail. It must also be glued properly—look for the blue primer at glued fittings.

PVC: This piping will look almost exactly like CPVC, but is not rated for hot temperatures and should not be used inside houses ever. You need to look at the listing on this pipe to tell the difference between PVC and CPVC. You generally never want to see PVC pipe inside the house: This is an indication of amateur work.

PB: This is a gray plastic tubing system that could be confused with PEX tubing. This product has a different chemical composition and has been known to break down due to chlorine in the water. Look for the label PB 2110. Be wary of this product; there have been class action lawsuits about this product alleging premature failure of both the tubing and many of the fitting systems. You will hear of this piping system as a "ticking time bomb," ready to burst at any time. (See left image on page 108.)

WASTE PIPES

While the specifics of waste piping are quite complicated, all of these specifics are attempting to ensure the same basic purpose: to safely and reliably carry wastewater out of the building.

Waste Piping Basic Rules of Thumb

- Waste pipes must slope to drain
- Waste pipes must be installed so that things don't become clogged
- Waste pipe traps should not be vulnerable to siphoning (this could allow sewer gas to enter the home)

Waste Pipe Materials

- ABS plastic
- PVC plastic
- Cast iron
- Galvanized steel
- Lead
- Copper

Waste Pipe Locations

I am often asked about adding a bathroom or finishing a basement to a home. The key is to add a bathroom that can connect to an existing waste piping system. Waste piping systems work with gravity. They are not pressurized. If you want to add or move a bathroom, you must think about where the waste piping systems are located and if a connection to an existing waste pipe is feasible.

Sewage Ejector Pumps

If you can't use gravity to connect to an existing waste piping system, there is an option called a sewage ejector pump. This is essentially a tank with a pump that can lift sewage out of the building. These are often used in basements where a bathroom has been retrofit below the sewer pipe that exits the house—thus a pump is needed to lift the sewage up to the sewer line.

Old Waste Piping

If you are buying an older home with old waste piping, you should know that repairs to this old piping could be needed at any time. Old waste piping is made from metal pipes, which are subject to internal corrosion. While the pipes may be working at the time of inspection, they could develop a leak at any time.

Old Waste Piping Red Flags

Look for rust stains and pitting on the pipe or below the pipes.

Average Life of Waste Pipes:

- **ABS/PVC:** Unlimited life if installed well and not physically damaged
- **Galvanized Steel:** 50 years
- **Cast iron:** Though harder to determine, I have seen this pipe last for 100 years or more, but lifespan is difficult to predict
- **Copper:** Also difficult to determine, this is a rare product, usually only found in 1950s and 1960s homes

Q: Why is there a P-trap below my plumbing fixtures?

A: The water in the trap prevents gas from the sewer line from entering the house.

Trap Terminology

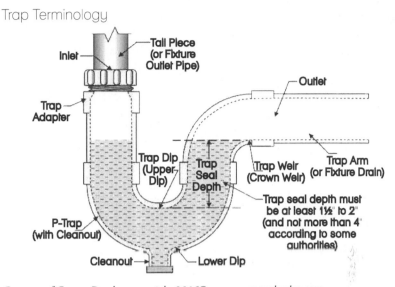

Courtesy of Carson Dunlop, copyright 2016©, www.carsondunlop.com.

A FINAL NOTE ABOUT PLUMBING AND WORKMANSHIP

Installing plumbing in a professional and reliable manner is harder than you might think. Licensed plumbers are right up there with licensed electricians as the most trained subcontractors who work on houses. Good plumbers tend to be expensive. For this reason, lots of homeowners take plumbing into their own hands. As home inspector, I am always on the lookout for amateur workmanship in plumbing systems. Spotting amateur workmanship can be tricky, but one tip I like to use is looking for barcodes on the plumbing—if I find them, I know the pipes likely came from the local hardware store as opposed to the plumbing supply store where many plumbers buy their supplies. So, if you are really interested in a house, look for barcodes on pipes and be sure to test your plumbing:

Is the hot side hot and cold side cold? Are faucets loose or well secured? Are shower pans sloped to drain? Are there leaks under the sink? You'd be amazed at what you can spot on your own if you just look a little.

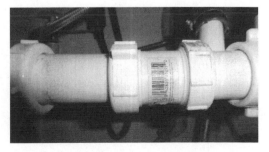

WINDOWS

My clients are always asking me about windows. I blame it partly on the slew of companies with large advertising budgets that work hard to convince homebuyers and homeowners that your windows need to be updated. In other words, there is money to be made in window replacements.

Window updating can transform an older house, but, while it is a great project, it can get very expensive and complex—you must consider how the new windows will tie into the exterior siding and interior mill-work. I like to make it clear to my clients that if energy efficiency is the sole reason for updating windows, there are usually more cost-effective ways to save energy.

Window Updating Facts

- The energy efficiency of windows is measured in U-value because windows are an assembly. However, if you want to simply measure the efficiency of a piece of glass, you can measure resistance to heat loss in glass using R-value. R-value is how we measure the depth of insulation in a house. In a modern attic in western Washington, insulation should be installed to R-49. Modern walls here have R-21 insulation in the bays between the wall studs. A single pane of glass is R-1. A double pane piece of glass is R-2 +/-. In short, windows are heat loss; even new insulated glass is a weak link in your thermal envelope. While updating windows will help your energy bills and your comfort, it may not help your bills as much as you think.

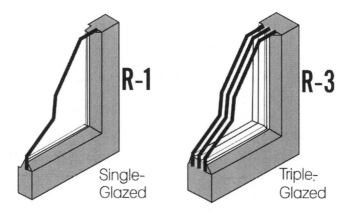

R-1 Single-Glazed

R-3 Triple-Glazed

- There are usually more cost-effective ways to improve the energy efficiency of your home other than updating windows. This is because windows are an expensive way to get limited R-value and limited resources can be targeted elsewhere with better payback. Some examples include a programmable thermostat for your heating system; low-flow aerators for sinks; sealant for air leakage in the building and ductwork; added insulation for attics and subfloors where accessible; and the installation of high-efficiency lighting, heating equipment, or energy efficient appliances.

When to Update Your Windows

- When they are rotting, in poor condition, or no longer open and close reliably
- When you feel they are unsafe: they lack modern safety glass[2] standards or proper egress in bedrooms[3]
- When the old single pane windows cause an uncomfortable chill in the winter and storm windows or curtains are not an adequate solution for you
- When doing larger renovation projects and it can fit into the budget. For example, if you have old clunky windows and you are also updating the siding, do the windows too

Q: Should I replace my windows if I am also doing the siding?

A: The answer is probably. This obviously adds a lot of cost to siding replacement, but your opportunity to replace windows in a quality and reliable way will come and go if you do not do them at the same time.

Q: What if some of the windows in a house have a cloudy appearance?

A: This is commonly called a lost seal and though this condition can become more or less apparent seasonally, a window with a progressed lost

---

2. Safety glass is like auto-glass—it shatters into innocuous fragments when broken.
3. Egress is safe passage in and out of the window so firefighters can get into the house to rescue people.

seal should be easy for anyone to spot. The most common ways to repair this condition is to replace the pane of glass inside the window frame, or replace the entire window, frame and all. The panes of glass can get expensive, so if you have old junky windows, consider updating the entire window. If the windows are in relatively good condition, plan on updating the glass. Be sure to count the number of panes because costs can be anywhere from $200 to $600 per pane of glass. If you have 10 lost seals, that can add up to $4,000 in a hurry! While there are some companies that offer to defog your windows, this does not work with tempered or laminated glass, but it can be a good option for larger expensive glass windows.

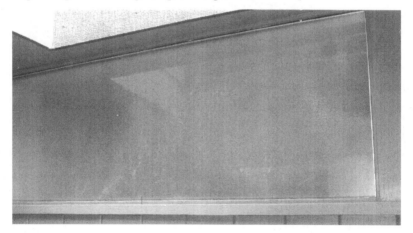

INSULATION: IN WALLS AND VAULTED CEILINGS

It's difficult to update or improve insulation inside walls and vaulted ceilings, and it is rarely cost effective unless you are doing a larger remodel or renovation project. This is because limited access makes updating expensive. Thus insulation in these tough-to-access locations is an "entrenched system." If you do retrofit insulation in a vaulted ceiling system, be sure the roof cavity gets ventilated properly. This could get tricky. If you are retrofitting insulation into wall systems of an old house, consider that there may be old knob-and-tube wiring in the walls that should not be buried in insulation. Be absolutely certain that all wiring is updated prior to insulating the walls, or this work could create a potential fire hazard.

VENTILATION

Having a properly ventilated house can be the difference between a dry house and a house with chronic moisture problems, so the importance of house ventilation cannot be underestimated. Remember, there is no more destructive force than water that works to damage our homes.

House ventilation is frequently misunderstood by homebuyers and homeowners. If a house has problems with ventilation, it can be confusing to determine what exactly is needed to correct the problem. Thus I consider ventilation an entrenched system. This section on ventilation will not make you an expert, but it will give you the knowledge and understanding you need to be an educated homebuyer and homeowner.

The first way house ventilation is confusing is that we ventilate lots of different things in different ways for different purposes. So let's start by thinking about venting two different places in the house:

1. Inside the thermal envelope of the house (your living space)
2. Outside the thermal envelope of the house, but still in your house. Think of these as the unheated cavities in the house like your attic and crawl space

INSIDE YOUR HOUSE AND MECHANICAL VENTILATION

Inside your house, it is important to use fan systems to discharge moist air to the exterior; this is called mechanical ventilation. A variety of sources contribute to interior moisture levels such as people breathing, showering, cooking, cleaning, and doing the laundry, as well as pets, plants, or aquariums. Moisture can also come from wet basements or crawl spaces. If left unchecked, moisture can accumulate inside a house and condense on cold surfaces. This can lead to molds and unsafe indoor air quality.

The relative importance of fan systems and ventilation in any given house will vary with five primary factors:

1. Region of the country

2. Time of year
3. Age of the house
4. Occupant behavior
5. Moisture problems endemic to a house (such as wet basements or crawl spaces)

Mold growing in an attic on the roof sheathing due to years of condensation.

Region: I will never forget my first day of classes in college. I was living in Colorado for the first time in my life and it was my second day in this new state. I woke, took a shower, went to breakfast, and then went to class. When I came back to my room before lunch, I went to put away my towel that was hanging over my chair. I became convinced that my roommate had covertly whisked my towel away to the dryer while I was in class. I had never known a towel to become dry just by leaving it out. This never happened to me in New England. Welcome to the arid West! The lesson here is that the urgency for venting moist interior air to the outside will change significantly based on where you live. For example, in desert climates, the air is dry, making it difficult to have high relative humidity problems inside a house.

Time of Year: In the summertime, it can be nearly impossible to control indoor relative humidity with fans and ventilation such as opening windows. For one thing, in some parts of the country, the outside humidity can be very high—so if you try and replace inside air with outside air using fans or opening windows, you just bring more moisture into the house. If you live in a part of the country that has a hot humid summer, the only way to dry the building is with air-conditioning or a dehumidifier.

Age of House: Old homes did not need fan systems because they leaked lots of air and had little insulation. Modern, energy-efficient homes need more mechanical ventilation to vent wet interior air outside, especially in the winter when cold walls, roofs, and windows present opportunities for condensing surfaces and chronic moisture problems.

Unfortunately, building codes never adopted a universal way to ensure adequate mechanical ventilation inside of houses, so different houses employ different strategies. These systems are almost never labeled. In fact, most homeowners don't even know that they have a mechanical ventilation system or that it is important. During your home inspection, be sure to ask your home inspector specifically about how the house you are looking at is designed to get its mechanical ventilation and if there are signs that more ventilation may be needed.

Occupant Behavior: Picture two identical houses, both 2200-square-foot houses built in 2010. Move a family of five into one and add an aquarium, two dogs, and a cat. Move a retired couple into the other with no pets. The family is home constantly, loves to cook pasta, and has no disposable income to travel. The retired couple spends every weekend at their cabin in the woods and likes to eat out. Which house do you think is likely to have a problem with high relative humidity? All of those family members breathing and showering and cooking and cleaning and doing laundry and the dogs panting and the aquarium evaporating—all these factors contribute to water being dumped into the house. The family house is much more likely to have indoor air quality problems resulting from high relative humidity, thus in a more urgent need of mechanical ventilation.

Chronic Moisture Problems: Sometimes, I can predict that a house has a problem with water in the crawl space when I am looking in the attic. If you see large mold blooms on the plywood of the roof deck inside the attic, there is a good chance the house has a wet crawl space—indicating that moisture is rising up through the house as vapor and condensing on the first cold surface that it hits. In wintertime, that cold surface is the cold roof decking. If a house has chronic drainage or moisture problems below the house, these need to be corrected to keep the building dry and safe. Often no amount of mechanical ventilation inside will be adequate until the drainage problem is resolved.

RED FLAGS INDICATING HIGH RELATIVE HUMIDITY PROBLEMS

What to Look for when Touring Homes

- Mold or condensation on the edges of windows

Many years of condensation around this window caused the framing in the walls to rot.

- Mold on the exterior walls inside closets
- Mold on the plywood decking of the roof in the attic
- Mold and/or condensation behind toilets or refrigerators

The bottom line is look for red flags indicating that houses have interior high relative humidity problems. If you see some of these signs, talk to your home inspector or a specialist (such as a mold remediation company) about common strategies used in your area to keep the building dry and look for signs that the house might have some larger drainage problems that are making the building chronically wet.

HOW CAN I MONITOR INDOOR RELATIVE HUMIDITY?

The best way to monitor indoor relative humidity (RH) is to buy a temperature and relative humidity gauge. The goal is to keep indoor RH below 50 to 55 percent in winter to reduce risks from condensation. When indoor RH exceeds 55 percent, use your fans: laundry fan, bath fan, and kitchen fan (while cooking). If running fans is not adequate, there may be a larger problem, such as a chronically wet basement, crawl space, or slab. You could also consider a dehumidifier or adjustments in occupant behavior, such as reducing the number of pets in the house, removing the aquarium and indoor plants, or opening a window during cooking. If you do not have reliable fans, you may need to install some quality fans.

Q: How do I mechanically ventilate the inside of my house?

A: Using fans is the key to reducing humidity.

1. The more the fan runs, the more air changes you get. You can also put these fans on a 24-hour timer so they come on automatically throughout the day. Be careful to avoid buying noisy fans, since you will not want to use the fan as often. Look for quiet, quality fans and also look for disabled fan timers—I see these all the time because home owners may have disabled the loud fan if it was driving them crazy.

2. You can connect a duct from the exterior to your HVAC system and run outside air into your house for make-up air, or fresh air. These systems are often called "fresh air" systems and usually run on a 24-hour timer to come on periodically throughout the day. These systems mechanically deliver outside air into the house through your HVAC

A disabled house fan timer will not help ventilate the house.

system. Heating and cooling contractors install fresh air systems like these.

3. Look for small vents in your windows that can be opened to allow a clean place for make-up air to come in. These can work in conjunction with your fans; your fans expel air outside and new air comes in through the vents in the windows.

4. The nicest system for mechanical ventilation is called a heat recovery ventilator. You don't see these often except in modern, well insulated homes. This is a heat exchanger that allows you to exchange exterior air for interior air without losing much heat because the warm outgoing air gives up its heat to the cool incoming air.

The inside of a heat recovery ventilator.

Q: What types of houses are especially prone to high relative humidity problems?

A: Generally, the 1970s ushered in our first attempts at tightening buildings. The 1980s through today are the most vulnerable since we significantly tightened buildings during this era. Homes from these eras that do not have forced air heating and cooling systems are especially at risk.

THE SUMMER FAN

Some parts of the country employ a summer fan. These are essentially large fans located in the attic that can be turned on at the end of a hot day to suck the heat out of the house and bring in the cool evening air. These are used for summer cooling purposes only.

OUTSIDE THE THERMAL ENVELOPE

Roof Cavity Ventilation

Venting your attic space and all roof cavities is important to prevent moisture build-up inside these spaces.

As a general rule, complex rooflines are difficult to ventilate well, and simple rooflines are easy to ventilate well. Ideal ventilation combines low "intake" vents like soffit or core vents with upper "outtake" roof venting like ridge vents or roof jack vents. This gives you convection—as the hot air rises out the top, it sucks in cooler air down low and you get a continuous airflow across the roof decking, keeping the wood dry. A complicated roofline often creates dead-air space, which means simple convective venting is sometimes inadequate.

This attic space will be difficult to ventilate due to the complex roofline.

Where to Look for Ventilation Problems

- Check front porch roofs and roofs that are also decks—venting here is often done incorrectly.
- Peek inside of soffit vents—they are often blocked by insulation or years of build-up of dust and organic material.
- In the attic, look for discolored plywood and framing—the wood ideally has a nice bright color as though it just came from the lumberyard.

Obstructed soffit vents.

123

The wood in this attic has a beautiful bright color like it just came from the lumberyard—a sign of a healthy house.

CRAWL SPACE VENTILATION

If you have a moisture problem in the crawl space below your house, and you have inadequate or blocked ventilation, you can quickly run into big problems. In these cases, water will sometimes be dripping off of insulation and concrete. This is a perfect recipe for chronic molds, rot,

The water is beading off of the insulation in this damp and poorly insulated crawl space.

and pest problems. Ideal crawl space ventilation is located in the corners since these are common dead-air spaces where condensation can occur.

What to Look For

- Are there vents for the roof and the crawl space?
- Do the vents look complete?

- Do you see soils or insulation blocking the vents?

Note: If there are no crawl space vents, the house is likely a slab on grade house or a basement.

Smart research for a homebuyer is asking your home inspector how your crawl space is ventilated and if it seems to be performing as intended. I would also want to know what the common ventilation procedures are for ventilating crawl spaces in homes in my area.

Crawl Space Ventilation Note

Depending on what part of the country you live in, the crawl space may or may not be ventilated. In places like the Southeast, with their warm and humid summers, they have found that ventilating crawl spaces causes moisture problems. In these areas, expect to find, "encapsulated crawl spaces," where the crawl space is brought inside the house.

CONCLUSION

As a homebuyer, you need to decide the type of house you are looking for and consider how much repair and maintenance you are willing to take on; there are no maintenance-free houses. Learning to see house systems through the core, entrenched, and disposable lenses will help you better measure your desires for maintenance against the realities of a given house you are considering. Houses that require extensive repairs to entrenched systems are more in the "fixer" category. In the next chapter, we will cover disposable systems and you will see the types of home maintenance, repairs, and updates that are at the heart of routine maintenance for just about any homeowner.

DISPOSABLE SYSTEMS 8

Every home has disposable systems: systems that need to be replaced over time because they simply wear out or break down. Many systems in a home fit into this category: hot water heaters, furnaces, boilers, roof coverings, gutters and downspouts, floor finishes, interior paint, exposed decks and porches, and appliances. If you have ever owned a house, there is a good chance you have tackled at least a few of these systems in your term of ownership.

A few systems that also fit under this category might surprise you: bathrooms, kitchens, skylights, and insulation (in both accessible attics and subfloors).

Let's explore what you need to know about all of these disposable systems and what to look for in each home.

Remember, the concepts here are designed to give you a comprehensive overview. This is not everything there is to know about these systems. Learning about these disposable systems means it will come as less of a shock to you if some of these systems need updating. When it comes to a home inspection, it is helpful to be able to see right through the need to update disposable systems. Almost all homes require updates to disposable systems—I like to think of these as spreadsheet items—a house that needs a new roof covering, water heater, or kitchen update, is not a bad house, it just has a few updates that need to be in the family budget.

HOT WATER HEATERS

Hot water heaters are usually tanks, though many people today are choosing tankless hot water heaters. Hot water heaters have a single task: to make your water hot. This is done with electricity, natural gas, propane, and occasionally, oil, solar power, or even wood.

Maintenance: Most tank hot water heaters have short useful service lives of 8 to 12 years. Most homeowners never do anything to their water heater until it breaks. If you want your water heater to last longer and perform more reliably, each year you should flush the tank, and, per the manufacturer's recommendations, replace the dip tube and the sacrificial anode.

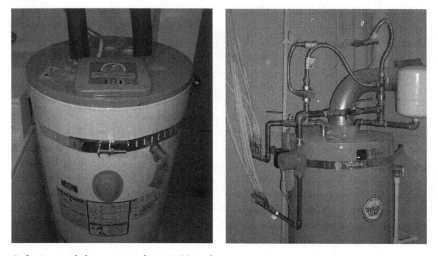

Left: A typical electric water heater. (Note the wire on top, running to the water heater.)
Right: A high-efficiency gas water heater. (Note the vent on top.)

Note: Water heater maintenance is ideally suited for the thrill-seeking retired engineer and though most homeowners will never do this, it does help extend the life of your tank.

TANKLESS

Water heaters without tanks are more efficient than those with tanks because they have efficient burners and they eliminate standing loss—the water that is heated in the tank but never used. On the other hand, heating hot water is only 10 to 20 percent of your total energy use for a typical house and these are very expensive water heaters. Will a tankless water heater pay for itself? It depends on your hot water use, but for a typical family in a typical house, there are usually better ways to increase energy efficiency.

If you want a tankless hot water heater, you need propane or natural gas. Electric tankless water heaters do exist, but they require a large amount of amperage and possibly an entirely new electrical service, so they are usually not practical.

Because tankless water heaters are a newer technology, we don't yet know how long they will last. My best guess: Anything that runs water through it constantly will have a tough time lasting a lot longer than 15 years, but the jury is still out. Manufacturers of tankless water heaters recommend regular flushing of the heat exchanges. I suspect that most homeowners do not perform this recommended maintenance.

HEAT PUMP HOT WATER

Heat pump hot water heaters are relatively new and yet untested. They use heat in exterior air to heat your water efficiently. If you encounter one of these, be sure it has an adequate supply of exterior air and is located in an "outdoor" space such as a garage. If it is located in a closet in the house, it will turn your closet into a meat freezer and your water heater will not work efficiently.

FORCED AIR FURNACES AND HOT WATER BOILERS

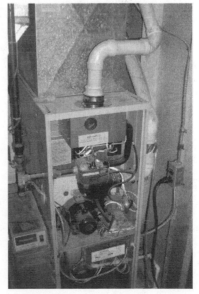

Boilers and furnaces are central heating systems.

Furnaces heat air to be distributed through the house using ductwork.

Boilers heat water, which is distributed through the house using pipes.

Boiler systems are generally more complex than forced air systems and they have the disadvantage of not being able to add cooling in most cases. Boiler systems can run water through floors to create radiant floor heating or through a variety of different radiator systems. Boilers can even use steam to heat radiators—a common installation in older buildings.

Older boiler systems are generally low-pressure systems and they were always kept separate from the domestic hot water that you use in sinks and showers. In some modern homes you may now see one hot water heater that heats *both* the house and the domestic hot water. Some of these systems are configured as open-loop systems, where the same water you drink could also have been run through your heating pipes. Be cautious about open-loop systems, these have a number of disadvantages:

1. The water in the system is more corrosive due to constant influx of new oxygen.
2. Stagnate water in heating pipes can lead to unsafe water in the domestic supply—think Legionnaires' disease.

Fuel Source: These central heating systems can be powered by natural gas, propane, oil, or electricity.

Heat Exchangers: An important concept to understand for any appliance that burns fuel to heat water or air is the heat exchanger. Every furnace or boiler you have will employ a heat exchanger of one

The inside of an old heat exchanger.

type or another. To understand a heat exchanger, visualize a welded clamshell of metal into which the hot flames from the burner are directed. This clamshell contains the products of combustion to be vented out a flue to prevent exhaust fumes from getting into your house. Air or water is then forced across the outside of the heat exchanger where the heat is transferred from the hot metal heat exchanger to the air or water in question. This is basically how all furnaces, boilers, and water heaters work.

Old heat exchangers were made from very thick metal and can often have long useful service lives: I've seen some old heating equipment still in service after 70 years. New heat exchangers are much thinner, more serpentine, and more complicated. They tend to last only 15 to 20 years. However, they are more efficient. With old heat exchangers, as much as

50 percent of your BTUs (British Thermal Units) would go out the flue—that's a massive amount of wasted energy.

General Rule: With heating equipment, we trade service life for efficiency—the more efficient the appliance is, the more complex it will be and the shorter useful service life it will have.

- Average life of modern forced air furnaces: 15–20 years
- Average life of modern boilers: 10–35 years
- Average life of older furnaces and boilers: 50+ years

HEAT PUMPS AND AC SYSTEMS

Heat pumps and air conditioners both do the same thing; they both move heat using a refrigerant cycle. The only real difference between a heat pump and AC is that AC moves the heat in only one direction—from the inside of your house to the outside. Heat pumps can move heat in both directions and are used throughout the heating and cooling year. For this brief overview I will discuss heat pumps, but all these principles are the same for AC systems.

To understand how a heat pump works, think of a refrigerator. A refrigerator does not make cold, it takes heat from an insulated box and dumps the heat into your room, resulting in the hot air you feel coming off your refrigerator.

Heat pump systems will generally have outdoor compressor units and most systems require an inside furnace or air handler and ducts through which heated or cooled air can pass.

Some new heat pump systems are ductless: These use outdoor compressors with an indoor unit but no ducts. These are not central heating and cooling systems, but they can be used to heat or cool your house and they are very energy efficient.

Heat pump systems can range in efficiency from roughly 100 percent efficient to nearly 400 percent efficient. This depends on the age and technology used in the system as well as environmental conditions such as outdoor air temperatures. Heat pumps are efficient because they do not make heat—they move heat—using electricity to run a compressor.

Most heat pump systems use air as the heat source; these are called air-sourced heat pumps and this is what you typically see when there is a compressor on the outside of the house. Geothermal heat pump systems are the most energy efficient because they use the ground as a heat source;

the ground is a very stable heat source compared to the air. For example, in Minnesota it could be negative 10 degrees Fahrenheit in the winter and there is not enough heat in that outdoor air to heat your home. But if you dig far enough into the ground, the temperature will still be 45 to 55 degrees—that is plenty of heat to use to heat your home using a refrigerant cycle, even when outdoor air temperatures are well below freezing

Note: The average life of a heat pump and AC system is roughly 15 to 20 years.

Heat pumps are my favorite heating and cooling system. Because they do both heating and cooling, they provide total thermostat-controlled comfort and they are very energy efficient. The downside is that they are an expensive piece of equipment to buy.

ELECTRIC RESISTANCE HEATERS

These come in five forms:
1. Baseboard heaters
2. Wall-mounted heaters
3. Central forced air furnaces
4. Electric pads installed in floors or ceilings
5. Heat lamps

Electric resistance heating appliances have a well learned reputation for being expensive heat sources. Resistance electric heaters like baseboards or wall-mounted heaters are actually 100 percent efficient and they are simple, nice little heaters. I like to think of them as toasters. Put a watt of electricity into an electric resistance heater and you will get the equivalent watt of heat back out. The problem with electricity is not the inefficiency of the heater, but the fact that you also need to pay for the two-thirds of the power that was lost in getting the electrons to your house. By contrast, if you deliver a fuel to your house such as natural gas, 100 percent of those BTUs (British Thermal Units) show up at your house; there are no distribution losses. The result is that electricity is an expensive heat source even if the heaters are 100 percent efficient.

In small condos and townhomes, electric heaters can be an ideal solution, but they are not well suited to heat large houses. You will often see electric heaters in additions where it was easier to add a wire and a simple heater than more ductwork. The predominance of electric heaters will change regionally; don't expect to find them as frequently in parts of the country with expensive electricity rates.

Be careful with electric heaters. Putting furniture, curtains, and electrical cords near these heaters is a fire hazard. Also, be sure to keep electric heaters clean.

Tip: To clean electric heaters, first turn off the power to the heater at the circuit breaker then use a can of compressed air to blow the dust off the heaters.

Also look to see if thermostats control the electric heating system. Electric heaters that are only controlled by a plastic knob are not going to keep you as comfortable as a system that is controlled by thermostats.

Electric heaters can last a very long time but eventually they get very dirty and unreliable. I would consider updating electric heaters every 20 years or so.

ELECTRIC PANEL

Like any mechanical device, electric panels and their breakers get less reliable as they age. Older electric panels may be functional but may also need to be updated for any number of reasons. The time for panel updating is often when you are doing a renovation to the house but you may also run into certain

Old fused panel.

Zinsco brand panel.

brands of panels that have a reputation for unreliability.

Watch out for old fused electric panels; most insurance companies will no longer insure homes with fused panels.

The 1960s through 1980s ushered in a number of poorly made and unreliable electric panels. If your home inspector finds one of these brands, it needs to be replaced: Zinsco, Federal Pacific Electric's Stab-Loc, and Bulldog Pushmatic are examples.

Note: Newer electric codes are going to add expenses to a new electric service as a nearly full suite of expensive arc fault protected breakers are starting to be required.

Permits: Look for permit stickers on updated panels—this is a good sign that tells you that a homeowner went through an appropriate permitting process when updating an electrical service, indicating that the workmanship is likely to be professional. If you are replacing an electric panel, pull permits with your local building department—an electrician can do this for you.

ROOF COVERING

Roof coverings come in many different types and styles and the predominance of any particular covering will change regionally. In hot desert climates, expect to see clay tile and concrete tile roofing systems; in cooler climates, expect to see composition shingle roofs; in snow country, expect to see metal roofs; and on a flat roof, expect to see some type of membrane system. It would be wise to become familiar with the roofing systems commonly used in your area and I would be generally suspicious of unique systems that are not widely installed in your area—there may be a good reason for that.

Service life: The useful service life of a roofing system can be as few as 10 years or as many as 100 years. Roofing systems that last longer than 20 years tend to be much more expensive and include clay and concrete tiles, slate, and metal. Thus, some high-end roofing systems are not really disposable at all—not if they last for 100 years.

For most of us, however, roofing systems are not going to last that long and even high-end concrete tiles and metal roofs have trouble lasting more than 35 to 40 years. One problem that even top-end roofing systems face is that the roof is only as good as its weakest link. Once the underlayment and fasteners and flashings start to wear out, it can become more expensive to repair an older roofing system than to replace it.

Here is a basic primer for useful service life of different roofing materials:

- Slate and Clay Tiles: as many as 100 years
- Concrete tiles, metal roofs, and high-end wood shake or wood shingles: 35+ years
- Asphalt composition shingles, most wood shake, and most membrane systems: 20 years

Here are the basics of what you need to know about roof coverings:

1. **Roofs fail where they start, stop, and change direction**. This means penetrations through roofs such as chimneys, skylights, valleys, and roof/wall junctures are very common problem areas.
2. **Localized leaks are not necessarily a chronic problem**. If a roof is leaking at one place, such as a chimney, it is possible that only a localized flashing repair is needed and not a complete roof replacement. However, this would need to be investigated further.
3. **Leakage in the "field" of the roof is a bad sign**. Such leakage cannot be associated with a specific penetration through the roof. This indicates incorrect installation and often requires a complete roof replacement to repair.

What to Look For

- Does the roof look new or old?
- Can you find leaks inside or at the eaves? Look around the eaves where the roof stops, under skylights, around the chimney and fireplace, by the electric panel, and at the base of a valley.

Q: Do you think this roof has a few more years on it?

A: Most often, many roofs can be made to last a little longer. If you are willing to tolerate a leak, you can patch it and repair it and drape tarps over it if you have to. The truth is that it is hard to predict if and when a roof will actually leak and a lot of what you are buying with a new roof is reliability.

The question you really want to be asking is if it will be cost effective to repair this roof or if you should just replace it. Part of the answer to this question is situational: If you are planning an addition to the house in 2 years, you probably want to do whatever you can to make that roof last another 2 years. If you have beautiful finishes in the house and the prospect of a leak keeps you awake at night and sends fear into the heart of your soul, it's time to get bids from a few roofing contractors. So the best answer to the most common roofing question is best answered based on one's own situation and risk tolerance.

GUTTERS AND DOWNSPOUTS

Don't underestimate the value of a reliable gutter and downspout system for protecting your house. You may not want them in snow country because the snow will rip them off your home every winter, and you may not want them in a desert because it just does not rain enough to matter.

But in most of the country, there is no substitute for a reliable gutter and downspout system. It is not uncommon to see expensive damage to buildings simply because the gutter and downspout system was left to fail.

Critical Gutter Maintenance: It is very important to keep your gutters clean and working well. This involves regular maintenance: scooping out built-up leaves and debris that accumulate. Look to see if the gutters look clean when touring a house—this is a great clue as to how the owner keeps up the house.

Common Types of Gutters

Seamless Aluminum: This is the most common gutter and downspout system and my personal preference. This system is cut to fit on-site, often by workers with a truck full of spools of aluminum stock in the back. This custom fitting reduces the number of seams in the gutters and makes for a stronger and more reliable gutter system.

Aluminum gutters and downspouts tend to last about 30 to 40 years. This matches well with the installation of a second composition roof—so I find gutters and downspouts tend to last for roughly the same period as two composition roofs. While one can repair leaking, clogged, and poorly sloped gutters and downspouts, there comes a point where it is more cost-effective to replace the gutters and downspouts entirely.

Tip: Coordinate an old gutter replacement *after* a roof is installed, because reroofing can damage your gutters with all of the ladders and compressor hoses and materials going up onto the roof.

Tip: Taking off old gutters and downspouts can be an easy do-it-yourself project as long as the gutters are not too high. You can remove the old gutters, repair and paint the fascia,[1] and then hire a company to install new gutters and downspouts.

Plastic: If you live in a place where it rains a lot, don't use plastic gutters and downspouts. Nearly every plastic gutter system leaks. These are not reliable long-term gutter and downspout solutions.

Copper Gutters: Copper gutters and downspouts are beautiful and reliable. If you have money burning a hole in your pocket, go for it!

---

1. The vertical frieze or board below a roof edge that often defines the roofline.

SKYLIGHTS

Ideally, skylights get updated with every new roof. I find they last about 30 years if installed well. This means if you have a roofing system that lasts 15 to 20 years, such as a composition shingle roof, you may have a problem with your skylight in the middle of the service life of the second roof. When replacing skylights, the flashings should be replaced as well. If the skylight is on a low-slope or a flat roof, use bubble style skylights that shed water. It is usually pretty easy to spot skylight leakage. While I occasionally find hard-to-spot skylight leaks, they are usually self-evident—just look inside the house around the skylights to see if they have been leaking. Slight water staining or localized molds and slight discoloration may be from seasonal condensation and/or UV exposure. Try not to confuse these minor red flags with more serious leakage problems.

Inspection Tip: It is always smart to look around skylights when touring a house to see if you can find signs of leakage.

INTERIOR FINISHES: FLOORS, WALL, AND CEILING PAINT

The quality and service life of interior finishes is subjective and fluid and is determined by owner behavior and expectations. I have seen the insides of new homes trashed in just a few years and I have seen homes from the 1950s preserved as virtual time capsules—a testament to diligent care and maintenance.

It cannot be understated that quality finishes are a luxury to some and a necessity to others. You need to decide which camp you are in. While most homes with nice finishes are also nice homes, you can pay a lot of money for quality finishes that do not reflect the bones of the house. One of the purposes of this book is to teach you to look at the bones of the house so you are not taken simply by the bling of the finishes.

Inspection Tip: Use the quality of the finishes to help you see the type of homeowner you are buying a house from: Was this homeowner tidy, sloppy, careless, neat? This tells you worlds about how the home was maintained.

PAINTING AND FLOORING

Repainting houses and installing new finish flooring is expensive. If you are in the market for a fixer, you probably know this and might even be planning on using sweat equity to redo these finishes. If you are a busy professional or part of a busy family and want quality finishes but have no time to make the upgrades, you want choose a house with finishes that meet your expectations or be willing to hire the appropriate contractors to help get you there.

The service life of flooring depends a lot on what materials were used and how well they were cared for. Hardwood floors that are ¾ of an inch thick and properly installed ceramic tile can last the life of the building if well cared for. Wall-to-wall carpeting, plastic sheet goods, and less expensive laminated wood flooring products have a difficult time lasting longer than 20 to 30 years.

APPLIANCES

Appliances are not to be trusted. Even the most expensive models of dishwashers and ovens can break in just a few years. The basic problem with newer appliances is that they are more complicated than older appliances—remember the guiding principle: simplicity is your friend.

I have come to approach new appliances with great apprehension. Manufacturers are continually adding futuristic features to the controls, muddying a process that is supposed to be helpful and efficient: washing machines with "play" buttons—since when did I "play" a load of laundry?—and dishwashers with colored laser beams of light indicating when the load is done—is it a UFO about to take flight? I am occasionally embarrassed during a home inspection when I am unable turn on such an appliance. One option many homeowners choose in the face of these expensive and fickle appliances is a Home Appliance Warranty Program. If you are skilled at calling 800 numbers and pushing buttons to connect with the appropriate department, then such a program might be for you.

Inspection Tip: Closely monitor dishwashers and washing machines during the home inspection; never fully trust anything that squirts water inside of your house for a living. If a dishwasher leaks during inspection, I often find the puddle at the end of the job—just as I am leaving.

Energy Efficiency Note: Despite my gripes about the fickle nature of modern appliances, it should be recognized that new clothes washing machines and new refrigerators are remarkably more energy efficient than their old-technology counterparts.

BATHROOMS

Bathrooms are expensive, especially if you hire a contractor to execute the whole project for you. Bathroom upgrades can be done for much less if you do the work yourself and are thrifty about fixtures and finishes. Many of the least expensive fixtures in bathrooms today last only 15 years: cheap faucets, mixing valves, and pressed steel sinks. Beautifully installed bathrooms from the 1920s are still around and have lasted with minimum upgrades.

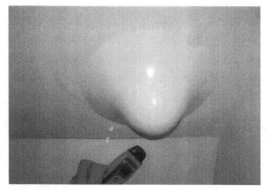

A leak from the bathroom is causing the paint to lift off the ceiling below it.

Bathrooms are a great place to look for water damage. If you are on the main floor, look at the ceiling for water stains since there may be a bathroom above you. Also look around the tub and shower enclosures and around the toilet.

The most complex and expensive thing to watch for in bathrooms are shower surrounds done in tile. Tile is difficult to inspect during a visual inspection because so much depends on what the tile is mounted on and what it is mounted with—neither of which are visible for inspection. In case you haven't noticed, a lot of water runs in your shower. Leaking tile in a shower can conceal hidden water damage and be a very expensive repair. Red flags to watch for: loose or cracked tile and displacement in tile indicative of amateur workmanship.

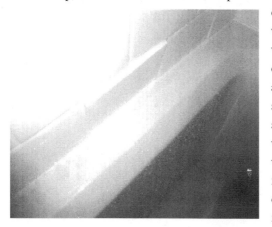

Note the displaced tile.

KITCHENS

Kitchens are also expensive—think death from a thousand cuts. There seems to always be just one more expensive thing you need to buy to finish off a kitchen. Kitchens and bathrooms are the high-cost areas of most homes.

You need to decide how important quality kitchens, bathrooms, and interior finishes are to your purchase decision. To some homebuyers, these are utilitarian places that just need to work. Other homeowners take great pride in the quality of the finishes in their home and spend thousands of dollars for luxury items. If quality kitchens and bathrooms are important to you and you like the ones installed in a particular house, those finishes will influence your purchase decision. However, this bling should not be confused with a house that has great bones. I have seen $100,000 kitchens installed in houses that I considered little more than cabins and there are a lot of homes that exemplify the lipstick on a pig comparison. So go in with your eyes wide open and do not be swayed by the beautiful finishes and fresh paint alone.

From a bones standpoint, the most important part of a kitchen is its role as part of the core system. If the kitchen is too small or the wrong shape or in the wrong location, it can be expensive to correct. If you like the shape, location, and light in the kitchen and you just need to update finishes, this is a simpler issue—a cosmetic problem.

INSULATION: INACCESSIBLE ATTICS AND SUBFLOORS

Attic

If the house has an easily accessible attic, adding attic insulation is one of the easiest and best ways to improve the energy efficiency of your house; you simply blow in more insulation.

Make sure the current insulation is not rodent-damaged, which would indicate a need for trapping, exclusion work, and possibly control of vegetation

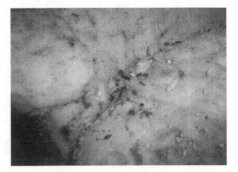

Rodent-damaged insulation.

around the house. Also watch for a type of insulation called vermiculite, which may contain asbestos.

Before adding insulation to an attic, remember that the new insulation will inhibit access to this space. Any wiring or fan projects should be finished before insulating. Once insulated to modern codes, you hope to not need to go up there again.

Vermiculite insulation.

Crawl Space Subfloor

When easily accessible, this insulation can also be updated. Updating subfloor insulation is more expensive because it is more labor-intensive as the "batting" (rolls of insulation) needs to be installed and supported by hand.

What to Look For

Fiberglass insulation in subfloors of crawl spaces is vulnerable to rodent problems—rodents love to nest in fiberglass insulation. If the house has a crawl space that cannot be sealed reliably and the building has a history of rodent problems, consider insulating with spray foam or rigid foam or even leave it uninsulated if you are in a mild climate.

EXPOSED DECKS

Be certain your home inspector checks any decks thoroughly, as poorly built and unsafe decks are common. A poorly installed deck is a safety hazard because it can collapse and even kill.

Look for a deck structure that is well built with pressure treated lumber. This lumber will last for several generations of decking. Softwood decking, like cedar and redwood, will last for 20 to 30 years, depending on exposure and care.

Plastic decking materials and hardwoods can last even longer, but they are more expensive to install. Most 20-year-old decks are likely to have a maintenance need of some kind.

Tip: A great website that shows everything you need to know about proper deck construction, including continuous load path, proper footings, flashings, ledger boards, lumber, and hangers is at http://www.safe stronghome.com/deck.

CONCLUSION

Given the relatively short useful life of some roofs, water heaters, furnaces, flooring, paint, kitchens, bathrooms, and other disposable systems, it is important to understand how they fit into the investment that is your house. The first thing you can do is identify how long many of these systems will last. For example, hardwood floors or clay tile roofs may last for your entire term of ownership and they represent a long-term investment in owning a lower maintenance house. Other disposable systems, such as three-tab shingle roofs, appliances, furnaces, and water heaters, may all require updating on 20-year schedules. Thinking of disposable systems in this way will help you create a realistic budget for maintenance and updating.

Many disposable systems are fundamental to the operation and maintenance of a home. Houses need roofs, water heaters, air conditioners, and furnaces—ongoing updating is simply a fact of home ownership that needs to be factored into your financial decision to become a homeowner and not a renter. Other disposable systems such as finishes, bathrooms, and kitchens don't last very long—possibly not even as long as your mortgage—and are essentially a luxury and a depreciating asset compared to the bones of the home. For example, you could buy a home with gorgeous paint, flooring, kitchens, bathrooms, and decks and 20 years from now, people will scoff at how dated it looks and laugh aloud about the faux brass-colored fixtures and the unreliable looking appliances. You need to learn to see the quality of these disposable systems when you look at houses and learn to compartmentalize how important these various systems and their quality and reliability are to you.

PART III

Using Alternative Sorting Methods

HOW OLD AM I? TAKE A GUESS!

Read on to find these houses in their respective sections, revealing their ages.

SORTING HOMES BY AGE 9

When looking at houses, one thing you should notice right away is that each decade is characterized by distinct architectural styles. I don't care where you are shopping for a house—there are local architectural trends and with a bit of research and a little practice you can learn to guess the approximate age of homes in your area. I'm spot-on most of the time—it has become a parlor trick of sorts for me and it can be a fun way to learn to really look at the homes and neighborhoods in which you are house hunting.

Once you have guessed the age of a prospective house, look around the neighborhood. Can you spot homes of similar age, or do you see a hodgepodge of different aged homes? This will help you start to "see" the neighborhood as the history of the area starts to come into focus.

The breakdown by decade that I have done in this book is based on my experience in the Pacific Northwest where I live. You will find similar trends in every town and city across America; the details and specifics will change regionally, but residential construction follows patterns that can be recognized when you learn how to break down construction visually by decade. These patterns can become invaluable tools when learning how to look at and compare houses.

KNOW YOUR HISTORY

You will be amazed how housing trends start to make sense when you understand what your town or neighborhood was like at the time the homes were constructed. This process will make you think about the local history around you and help you be a more invested homeowner as you become aware of the forces that shaped your community.

Example 1: I live on an island in the Puget Sound that for years was little more than a difficult-to-get-to rural farming community with strawberry farms, fishermen, and summer cottages.

After the nearby emergence of economic powerhouses like Microsoft, Starbucks, and Amazon ,coupled with a top-ranked public school system, this island became prosperous. Many people relocated from California or the East Coast, expecting a trove of beautiful older housing stock. They are often surprised when they learn that the million dollar waterfront house they are looking at actually began as an old, hand-built weekend home, puzzled together from five different additions and remodels, and, in fact, is not very well constructed.

Example 2: The most expensive and prestigious homes today are built on the waterfront. But go back 100 years and wealthy people built their homes on much more sensible locations: at the tops of hills, where they would be safe, dry, and well defended. It was the working class who lived on the water with Queequeg and the other sea-fearing riffraff of the day. Even the term "skid row" derives from the waterfront area in Seattle, where tree logs were skidded down the hills into the water for processing into lumber.

Clearly, our point of view has changed as to what makes a quality building lot, and so the location of where nice homes are built has also changed. You may be surprised where you find well constructed historic homes in your community. Occasionally, I find myself inspecting a home in an economically disadvantaged section of town and I realize that I am looking at a surprisingly well built house. That means the neighborhood was likely prosperous at one time, but later fell on hard times. The cause can often be traced to the expansion of a new highway or nearby airport construction.

It is advantageous to become an educated home shopper or homeowner by learning about the trends of your community. Experienced Realtors and home inspectors can be great resources to understand local trends and should be able to help you. You can also see if there is a local historical society or museum.

Tip 1: When thinking about the history of houses, go to the building department and see if they have any permit history or records of additions, wiring work, or structural modifications. Do they have any site plans that might show critical areas or wetlands for the property you are looking at?

Tip 2: Look for a C.L.U.E. report on a property. These are essentially a seven-year look-back to see if any insurance claims have been made against the property. This could indicate prior water damage or fire damage.

Tip 3: Consider when boom times have happened in construction. Housing construction booms tend to result in more hastily constructed homes. The 1930s is a decade when not much was built because of the recession, the homes that I do inspect from that era tend to be well built. By contract, whole communities seemed to spring up in the 1990s and some of this construction is pretty shoddy.

Here's an historical look at houses and home construction trends in the Pacific Northwest, specifically, in the Greater Seattle area. You may have housing in your area that is older than this. I suspect that many of the trends you read about here will hold true for even older houses, but this is where having a home inspector and Realtor who are knowledgeable about the homes in your area will be a great asset.

1880s—TURN OF THE CENTURY

At the end of the nineteenth century, Seattle was largely undeveloped and most of what was constructed from the 1880s to 1900s has burned or fallen down by now. As a result, we don't see many houses that are older than the 1880s and anything older than the turn of the century is rare.

Interestingly, neighboring cities, such as Tacoma, have much nicer housing stock despite the fact that it is now a less affluent city. Below is an article that illustrates the politics and economics that drove construction and housing during this era. Again, understanding your local history can really help you better understand your local housing stock.

Northern Pacific Railroad announces Tacoma terminus on July 14, 1873

On July 14, 1873, an expectant crowd gathers at Yesler Mill in Seattle to hear Arthur Denny (1822–1899) read a telegram from Northern Pacific Railroad executives R. D. Rice and J. C. Ainsworth announcing the railroad's decision on where to locate the terminus. The crowd expects the terminus to be located in Seattle, but Denny opens the telegram and reads, "We have located the terminus on Commencement Bay." Seattleites are shocked, dismayed, and angered that the planned transcontinental railroad and its coveted wealth of goods and passengers would serve Puget Sound not from Seattle but from Tacoma, then barely a village. The reaction in Tacoma is quite the opposite—celebration. Promoter Matthew McCarver had platted Tacoma City on Commencement Bay speculating that the railroad would come there and his investment proved a good one.

The summer before, Northern Pacific Railroad officials spent a week touring Puget Sound in a steamboat looking at sites for a terminus. Various towns got into a bidding war over it. Seattle offered the Northern Pacific 7,500 town lots, 3,000 acres of land, $50,000 in cash, $200,000 in bonds, and the use of the shoreline for tracks and a depot.

The railroad started building a line from Kalama on the Columbia River north toward Puget Sound. Ainsworth and Rice, charged with locating the terminus, decided on Tacoma, which was scarcely a village, because it was closer to the Columbia River and required the least amount of track to be laid. They delayed making the announcement until they secretly purchased as much of the land at Commencement Bay as they could, some distance from McCarver's Tacoma City. The Northern Pacific called its settlement, New Tacoma.

The outraged Seattleites started building their own railroad, which eventually reached the King County coal town, Newcastle. This became the Seattle & Walla Walla Railroad, governed by a company whose trustees were some of Seattle's most prominent businessmen: Arthur Denny (1822–1899), John Collins (1833–1871), Franklin Matthias (1826–1891), Angus Mackintosh, Henry Yesler (1810–1892), James McNaught (1842–1919), John. J. McGilvra (1827–1903), James M. Colman (1832–1906), and Dexter Horton (1825–1904).

Tacoma City and New Tacoma would later unite and become Tacoma. The Northern Pacific's decision to locate the terminus at Tacoma began a long, antagonistic struggle between the railroad giant and the optimistic, but still very young city of Seattle.[1]

On the East Coast, in the Southeast, and in the Midwest there is a wealth of fabulous housing stock from this era. The late 1800s was the height of Victorian style home building (large, almost mansion-like homes). This reflects the great wealth that was being accumulated in the New World at this time as railroads expanded and residential development flourished.

Today these sophisticated Victorian homes can be found in cities, in the country as estates, and in rural areas as farm homes.

Structure

If you are looking in an area prone to earthquakes, these homes are likely to be seismically weak compared to 1970s and newer buildings since there were no seismic standards when they were built. The advent

---

1. This comes from historylink.org, Essay 922.

of poured concrete was brand new in this era, so expect a hodgepodge hof foundations, possibly built from stone, brick, block, and/or sections of updated foundation. This era also marks the rise of the circular saw and machine-made nails, thus the era of timber framing came to an end, replaced by "balloon framing."

Balloon Framing: Balloon framing is a style of framing that is distinguished from modern platform framing. In platform framing, you build one story, then rest the second floor on top of the wall to the first floor. In balloon framing, the walls may span from the first floor all the way to the top of the second floor and then the middle floor is attached to the walls in between.

Site Work

Put yourself in this turn-of-the-century era and try to imagine what it took to excavate a building site. You are likely using shovels and pick axes. Note to self: Expect marginal site work. This means the building is more prone to differential settlement and drainage problems. On the other hand, if you were building a house this long ago, you may have had your pick of top-notch building lots. Sometimes, homes from this era are on the best building sites in the community. Great building sites are sometimes more forgiving of inadequate site preparation.

Framing

The farmhouse-type structures from this era are often humble and prone to overspanning and inconsistent framing practices. If you remember from chapter 5, overspanning is when dimensional framing lumber is run over too long a span. This can make a framing system such as a floor, ceiling, or roof sag, deflect, or even crack under loads. Think of deflection as bouncing or bending under loads.

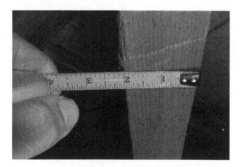

A real 2 × 10 board. Such framing lumber today is actually only 1½ inches thick.

Despite the availability of quality old growth lumber back then, not everyone could afford nice lumber when building their home. The nicer homes from this era have gorgeous old-growth lumber structures that were carefully built by crafts-men. Everything was dependent on the quality of the builder and the amount of money the owner had to build the property at the time.

Tip: When house hunting, look for the quality of the lumber used to determine whether an old house was built by someone on a budget or someone with money to spend. Some of the best historic homes were built by early timber and railroad barons or successful local entrepreneurs of their time.

Core Systems

Homes from this era should have updated systems. The advent of electricity was somewhat new to the world, which means there wasn't much to plug in. That also means the original wiring system for these homes would be inadequate for today's modern family.

The heating system would also be primitive and well past its design life now. It is common to see central heating systems installed in these homes today—these systems are likely retrofit from the original build. You may find as many as five or six fireplaces in different rooms in these homes, a relic that predates the central heating system. Also, look for an old abandoned coal shoot where coal was dropped down into the base-ment for heating. Homes from this era are likely to have little or no insu-lation, single pane windows, and galvanized steel piping. In short, you should look to see what has been updated. Any disposable system that is original should be considered obsolete and suspect.

1900–1920s

These first two decades of the twentieth century are characterized by craftsman-style homes. Many of the quality versions of this era have tremendous character with large roof overhangs and well protected old growth wood siding. In contrast, you can expect cabins, farmhouses, and fisherman's homes from this era to be humble and poorly built.

Foundation and Structure

Structure is likely to be a concern. Many homes from this era have post and pier foundations. Common, too, are foundations with no real footing system as well as hodgepodge foundations with some poured con-crete, some brick, and some block. The great San Francisco earthquake and fire of 1906 destroyed almost 80 percent of that city and resulted in

a shortage of concrete along the entire West Coast. As a result, you may see a lot more post and pier foundations on the West Coast after 1906.

Look for homes that are half basement and half crawl space. Often the two parts of the foundation settle relative to each other because the footings for the basement are much deeper and on more compacted soils than the footings for the crawl space.

Site Work

Expect site work to be marginal at best. Often crawl spaces are poorly excavated.

Systems

Due to the age of the home, you should be concerned about building systems such as heating, wiring, and piping. One of the first things you should do is look at the systems in the home. When I am looking at these, I like to distinguish if the home has been

1. Systematically updated as part of a large project at one time. What was the quality and scope of this project?
2. Patched together over the years. How well was this done?
3. Original, or close to it, with minimal upgrades.

Note: In 1908, Sears, Roebuck & Co. rolls out a kit house, available in its catalogue.

1930s

The 1930s is an interesting decade because it is in the middle of the Great Depression. Very few houses were built during the Great Depression but the ones that were were typically by people with money. I have found that many of these homes are well built with beautiful framing lumber, decent foundations for their age, and stunning architecture, usually with a blend of art deco and Tudor styles.

What to Expect

- Look for updated wiring, plumbing, and heating systems. Original wiring and plumbing systems will not perform reliably given their age.
- There should be a poured concrete foundation. Site work is sometimes marginal.
- Check old, wood-framed single pane windows: This was the height of beautiful leaded glass window installations. Some of the windows from this era are beautiful, but may be deteriorating where exposed to the weather.
- Tudor homes from this era have steep roofs—good for shedding water, but not much in the way of roof overhangs. Expect old

155

wood windows, siding, and trim on exposed sides to be rotted and expect the need for siding work if it has not already been done.

- Lots of brick siding was done in this era—look to see if it has been repointed or repaired, and look for step cracking and corrosion or damage at steel lintels. (Remember that repointing or tuck pointing brick is replacing the mortar between the bricks.) (See image on page 89.)

- Buried oil tanks may be present—this was a common heat source. A title search may disclose this, but often you need to look around the property and inquire with the seller or the local fire marshal. (See chapter 16 for more information about buried oil tanks.)

WAR ERA—1940s

Homes from the 1940s, sometimes referred to as war boxes, as a reference to homes that were built during and after World War II, are typically small, one-story houses with simple rooflines and no roof overhangs. It is the lack of the roof overhang that gives them their boxy feel. Many of the houses have hip roofs and masonry chimneys.

The 1940s is when foundation work started to be more consistent and reliable. It is also an era with quality lumber and good dry potential. (See chapter 15 for more on dry potential.) The best of these homes are quite durable.

- Small square footage from these homes. Think simple, humble houses.
- The need for siding maintenance on exposed sides, due to age and lack of roof overhangs.
- Usually built from nice old-growth wood materials.
- The need for properly working gutters; this is especially important when there is no roof overhang because entire walls can rot out from failing gutters that spill water down the siding.
- It's typical for the old storm drain system to perform inadequately. Because of this, the basement or crawl space could have drainage problems.
- War era houses with basements tend to be less prone to settlement because the footings are deeper and more likely to be on well compacted soils.
- Lead and asbestos, since these were common in paint and building materials from this era.
- Old buried oil tanks or even current oil heat.
- No seismic work to have been done originally. Ask, "Has the house been retrofitted?"
- Original wiring and plumbing will be unreliable. Look for signs of updated pipes and wiring or expect the need to do some updates yourself.
- Air-conditioning, having been born, starts opening hotter parts of the country to development.

1950s AND 1960s

The mid-century modern house era spans roughly from the 1950s to the 1960s. This is one my favorite few decades of home construction, particularly when I find a well built specimen.

These small windows just below the low slope roof are called clearstories.

Classic 1950s.

The designs of the day tend to feature more open floor plans than older houses. Expect more windows and glass, since there was an effort to bring the outside in. Designs started featuring more flat roofs and some homes have great roof overhangs, which protect the siding.

History

- Construction of the Interstate Highway System changed many communities as our country's main highways started to bypass many small towns.
- The 1950s is the decade when knob-and-tube was phased out. By the 1960s, we should be well out of the knob-and-tube era. Some houses in the early 1950s will be first generation of modern NM cable-style wiring. (See chapter 7 for more on wiring.)
- Electric service panels start moving from fused panels to modern breaker-style panels.
- By the end of the 1960s, we begin regularly seeing three-wire, grounded wiring. Before then, expect to see two-wire wiring systems in residential construction.
- 1965: Start of single-strand aluminum wire on 15 and 20 amp circuits. Runs through roughly 1975. This was most prominent from 1972 to 1975.

- You may find original heating equipment from this era. Furnaces and boilers from this era were often well made, but not energy efficient. The price of a barrel of oil in 1960 was roughly $2.88. These will be at the end of their reliable design lives and expensive to continue to operate.
- The 1950s and 1960s are the start of the plywood era. Before then, more of house sheathing was done in shiplap-style solid wood. While laminated wood in some form has been around for years, it was not until after World War II that plywood manufacturing of softwood started to grow rapidly in the United States. By the 1960s, plywood was starting to be used almost exclusively for sheathing and decking in residential framing.
- End of the era when you might to find hardwood floors below shag carpet. This, "lucky find," is most common in 1950s and 1960s houses.

- The best specimens have fabulous old growth wood siding, which is protected by roof overhangs.
- You are more likely to find homes with great roof overhangs protecting the building.
- Houses in this era tend to have large yards compared to newer homes.
- Many homes from the era are ramblers (one-story homes).

1970s

One of my friends calls the 1970s the "cocaine years." The 1970s were an interesting decade because some of the construction practices were quite good, but some of the designs were a bit eccentric. Perhaps the architects were watching too much of the Woody Allen movie *Sleeper*?

In the 1970s, we start to see generally better site work and poured concrete foundations are more reliable. This decade still has some nice

Photo courtesy of Frank Jenkins.

lumber and quality plywood. Plumbing tends to be copper, which can have a long service life where water is soft.

With the exception of single-strand aluminum, wiring is generally closer to modern standards than our older houses and may not need much in the way of significant updates or repairs.

Some of the architecture lacks roof overhangs. This construction often has a modern flair with tall exposed walls of wood siding and angular glass windows. While quality siding products may have been used on these buildings, weather exposure combined with age can create exterior maintenance issues on these buildings.

History

- **Asbestos:** In 1978, Congress prohibited use of asbestos in building materials. They did not prohibit sales of existing materials, however, so you could find materials containing asbestos in homes into the early 1980s. You need to test to verify. (See chapter 16 for more information on asbestos.)
- **Energy Codes:** It was the energy crisis of the 1970s that spawned our first energy codes in Washington. There are exceptions in some states, but generally the 1970s gave us the birth of the modern energy code. In Washington State, 1979 ushered in a big change in energy codes with double pane windows and significant increases in insulation.
- **Lead:** 1978 was also when Congress prohibited adding lead to paint. Expect that homes built prior to 1978 will have lead in the paint and possibly other building materials.
- **GFCI:** In 1971, GFCI's (Ground Fault Circuit Interrupters) code was required for outlets near swimming pools and exteriors. Throughout the 1970s, GFCI protection became required in bathrooms, garages, and exterior locations.
- **Insulated Glass:** Insulated glass (double pane glass) starts being used more frequently. Insulated glass was invented in the 1930s, but was fairly uncommon in most parts of the country until after the energy crisis.
- **Seismic Design:** Seismic design becomes code in areas prone to earthquakes.

What to Watch For

- Single-strand aluminum wiring
- Unreliable electric panels (brand names include Zinsco, FPE, and Bulldog PushMatic)
- Exposed envelopes—look for failing wood siding
- First generation double pane windows or single pane metal-framed windows
- Caution: You also may encounter disco balls, orange shag carpet, and mirrors over the bed so proceed at your own risk!

1980s

The 1980s represents the first generation of problems associated with trying to air-seal our houses and make them tighter and more energy efficient. After 9 years of tightening and creating rot and indoor air quality problems, the Indoor Air Quality Act was born (1989). The basic problem is that the newly tightened houses often suffered from chronic high relative humidity problems.

Photo courtesy of Frank Jenkins.

Photo courtesy of Frank Jenkins.

History

- Insulated glass and double pane windows are now the norm
- The rise of the modern vinyl framed window
- 1978 was the birth of OSB, which was not used widely until the 1980s
- Large houses begin appearing in the suburbs on large cul-de-sac lots
- The beginning of 2 × 6 wall construction

1990s

From an historical context, I think of the 1990s as the transition decade where we went from the way we used to build homes to the way we build them today. This was the "change decade" for new home construction.

Photo courtesy of Frank Jenkins.

Durability

From a durability standpoint, we ran out of quality inexpensive lumber to build with and started moving toward engineered wood products. OSB and MDF became more widely used. These products are not as decay-resistant as old growth lumber or plywood. We also started insulating and air sealing homes to create tighter and more energy-efficient houses. The downside is that this reduces dry potential in the building and creates buildings that are more susceptible to trapped water and water damage.

Systems

Many new systems were rolled out in the 1990s:

- New plastic plumbing products (PEX, PB)
- New siding products (LP, Hardboard, EIFS)
- New building wraps (housewraps such as Tyvek)
- New high pressure hydronic heating systems
- New electric heaters (Cadet)
- First generation, high-efficiency furnaces

While some of these new products can be seen as innovations and many were highly successful, others were failures and could even be classified as total disasters.

The lesson to be learned here is to be wary of new technology. Being cautious about technology can cut two ways. The downside is that home inspectors and building officials, wary of new technology, can stifle innovation. On the other hand, being cautious and creating reliable building standards has resulted in some of the safest construction in the world. The unfortunate reality is that if something has never been done before, how do you know how it will perform? This same principle applies to new construction: If it is brand new, how do you know how it will perform?

There was a very nice home I was inspecting on the east side of Seattle—expensive and built by a reputable contractor. It was a large house with synthetic stucco siding on the front, LP siding on three sides, wood windows that were exposed to the weather on two sides and a wood shake roof. See any red flags? Before I even walked inside, I knew that the house would need a new roof, new windows, and new siding. Wow! $80,000 later, I stepped inside to continue the inspection.

My best advice when looking at houses from the 1990s is to be especially wary of homes that have not had some updates. These homes are likely to have good structures and good wiring, but you are hitting a 20-year life cycle with many systems. When combined with a few recalled or failing products or systems intrinsic to this era, these homes can require significant investment to bring them up to date and make them reliable. But remember, this does not make a bad house! This just means that homes built in the 1990s are likely to need updates and repairs to many disposable systems and possibly some of their entrenched systems. In a good version of one of these homes, even an extensive repair list may not be a complicated repair list. Also note that as the years go by, these homes will have been updated and then the 20-year life cycle will be hitting the 2000s era houses. Life goes on and so does house maintenance.

Examples of 1990 Recalls and Problem Products

- LP siding
- Weyerhaeuser siding
- Masonite siding
- EIFS siding
- PB water supply piping
- Cadet heaters
- Consolidated furnaces (California)
- Apache ABS waste piping

2000s

The 2000s are the start of what I consider the new construction era. Foundations and wiring should all be permitted and recently inspected by city building officials (this does depend on where you live). Waste piping should be modern ABS or PVC and should have been installed by a licensed plumber. Windows should be new and insulated (double pane) glass and, if installed correctly, should not be leaking. Siding systems are leaning toward more reliable fiber-cement siding.

Photo courtesy of Frank Jenkins.

What to Watch For

- **Pre-Primed Spruce:** Many buildings from this era have exterior trim done in a pre-primed spruce. This product has no natural resistance to wood decay and rots easily—expect some rot repairs for exposed sections of trim.
- **Kitec:** Some of the hydronic hot water heating systems are using problematic plastic tubing (Kitec). (See right image on page 108.)
- **Open-Loop Systems:** This is the birth of the open-loop hot water and heating system that is widely accepted but somewhat controversial. (See the heating section in chapter 8 for more information.)
- **Envelope/Water Problems:** Check around windows and doors on the inside of the house.

Rule of Thumb: On older homes, I worry about the age of old systems and structure problems. On newer homes, I worry about moisture problems. This is a good general guiding principle.

CONCLUSION

I hope this chapter has given you some interesting insights on how you can use age to look at houses and predict what their respective attributes and shortcomings will be. Remember that all houses have distinct design advantages and disadvantages and understanding how these break down by age can help you narrow your home search and get your expectations in better alignment with the houses you are looking at.

SORTING HOMES BY HOME OWNER 10

Did you ever drive by a home and think, *that's a grandma house*, or, *I bet an engineer lives there?*

As a home inspector, looking at homes from every angle helps fully assess not only if it's a "good" house or a "bad" house, but whether it really is a fit for the person or family buying the home. I cannot underestimate the importance of this. *Every home is a great home for the right buyer if they can get it at the right price.* I almost never inspect a house that I think nobody should buy at any price.

With this in mind, a great way to look at houses is to think about them in terms of the occupant. In other words, learn to sort homes by the type of owner. This is both an illuminating and sometimes amusing way to quickly orient yourself to the type of home you are looking at. Over the years, I've created the following homeowner stereotypes. These categories should be taken lightly, but they can be surprisingly telling in explaining the type of maintenance list I put together during my inspection. My categories include the grandma house, the flipped house, the foreclosure/bank-owned home, the retired engineer house, the busy family house, the rental, the new construction, the artist's house, the reality TV house, and the builder's house.

Obviously there are many homes that do not fit into any of these stereotypes, so if you develop a new one—great! When houses do fall under a homeowner stereotype that you have created, you will find yourself more quickly oriented to the repair and maintenance list that may follow.

THE GRANDMA HOUSE

Why do I love grandma houses so much? Because a good grandma house has solid core systems and has been well cared for, despite needing updates to disposable systems and some entrenched systems.

Buying a grandma house does require a buyer who wants to put their mark on the place and has the budget and desire to make the upgrades and improvements needed. But if you get a good grandma house with good bones, you can renovate with new systems and you will have a sturdy, reliable home. Also, a grandma house does not typically try to hide anything: What you see is what you get.

- **Ideal grandma houses** have little or no deferred maintenance that is damaging the building. They have original, nice and simple rooflines without strange additions. Ideally, at least a few of the disposable and/or entrenched systems have been updated well. The home may need new flooring, new bathrooms, new water pipes, a new furnace, and a new water heater, but think of these as "spread sheet items." As discussed earlier, these types of repairs and updates are not indicative of a bad house; you just need to write a check to correct them. This process allows you the opportunity to put your stamp on the house. The good grandma house is often the perfect fixer-upper.
- **Lesser grandma houses** have deferred maintenance that is damaging the building as well as signs of on-going amateur workmanship to both core and entrenched systems. On some of these homes, you may need to redo some recent work if it was done poorly.
- **Bad grandma houses** have chronic problems with core systems. Deferred maintenance is damaging the building and there are years of "Larry The Cable Guy" repairs to the house that need to be peeled back. These may even have "unfortunate additions" done in the past that only add dysfunction. Even though what you see is what you get, you are not getting much.

Beware of a Change in Occupant Behavior

When inspecting a grandma house for a new young family, there are three things to watch out for: kitchens, bathrooms, and wiring.

These systems may work well for a grandma, but put these same systems under the stress of a modern young family and they fail. That's because a grandma puts significantly less stress on the home's systems than a young family does.

While a home inspector may test these systems and find they work, I am always afraid that these old systems will not respond so well to the rigors of daily family use. My advice is that you should expect that this can happen—old stuff that worked during inspection may stop working so well once you move in.

THE FLIPPED HOUSE

Flipped houses are the most likely houses to fall under the category of what you see is *not* what you get. Remember, a professional investor whose goal is to maximize his or her return on investment is often the purchaser of these homes. Their incentive is to do as little as possible while making it look like they did as much as possible. Because of this, the flipped house can be my least favorite type of home to inspect. Why am I wary of flipped homes?

1. **Hidden problems.** A home inspection is a visual inspection and there is a lot that a home inspector cannot see. When inspecting a flipped house, I start looking for signs that workmanship was amateur or incomplete in nature. If I see this, I start to worry about what I cannot see: What did these people touch? What has been done poorly, covered up, or left incomplete that I cannot see? Where do the repairs that need to be made begin and end? For example, let's say there is a loose and leaky kitchen faucet, two leaking waste pipes below bathroom sinks, a loose shower mixing valve, and a poorly mounted toilet. These are simple repairs, so why weren't they done? What else did they leave incomplete that I *cannot* see?

2. **Not inspected.** Remember, unlike new construction, much or all of the work that gets done in a flip typically has not been inspected by local building officials. Often, flipped homes are marketed as "everything is new," but it often takes an experienced eye to determine if this is true and if these new things were installed reliably. Even then, an experienced eye can be deceived if things have been intentionally hidden or covered up.

3. **Reliability.** With flipped houses, there is little standing between you and lipstick on a pig. If the city building officials did not check it, how do you know if the work is reliable? If the work is new, how do you know how it will perform? There is a reason why new construction comes with warranties. Use the clues uncovered during the home inspection to try and understand how reliable the new work will be.

The Good Flip

Not all flipped houses are bad! Over the years I have worked with some fantastic investor flippers. These are kind and knowledgeable people who enjoy the lifestyle of self-employment and take pride in what they do. They want to use their skills to deliver to the public safe and restored homes that are reliably and professionally remodeled. When inspecting a flipped house, the key is to decipher three primary things:

1. What is the quality of the work that was done?
2. What was the scope of the work that was done?
3. What was the core of the house like before they bought it? Were core and entrenched systems failing and then covered up during remodel work, or were they evaluated and addressed?

If the core and entrenched systems of the house were good, or if repairs were made to these systems, this is great. The bad flip focuses on the cosmetic stuff—things you can see—and ignores important repairs to core and entrenched systems.

An example of a good flip was a house I inspected recently. It was a 100-year-old house with a brand new foundation; this indicated the owner was willing to make the investments needed to ensure they were delivering a sound product when they were done. Good flips can be fantastic because they should have brand new systems and should have been cohesively updated. While this type of work is expensive, people who provide good flipped homes are often able to execute these repairs in a professional and cost-effective way.

The Bad Flip

Many flipped houses are in serious distress when purchased by an investor. This means only a small percentage of these distressed homes are the "cosmetic fixers" that most flippers are looking to buy. Believe it or not, many people who flip homes for a living do not hire a home inspector. Instead, they will have their "contractor" walk through the house looking for the window dressing items.

Bad flips usually start out bad: an investor overpaid for a lousy house. Then you notice that repairs lack a logical sequence and are incomplete or unprofessional. You then discover needed repairs to core or entrenched systems that went unrepaired—such as a drainage problem in the basement even though it has new wall-to-wall carpeting. This means pulling back "completed work" to access repair items—two steps forward and two steps backward.

Beware of Newly Finished Basements

Newly finished basements drive me crazy. On a dry summer day most people will see this: new paint, finishes, and new carpet. But all I can think about is what will happen to this basement when it starts to rain?

The first thing to check is to see if any waterproofing was done. If you see new finishes in old basements with no waterproofing on a flipped house, be warned: You need to expect the unexpected. Can you smell mold or stale air? Can you find an unfinished area where you might be able to get some clues as to if water has been a problem?

THE FORECLOSURE/BANK-OWNED HOUSE

I was hired to inspect properties for a woman who had done quite well for herself buying homes at foreclosure auctions, then fixing and flipping them. I asked her how this worked and what the trick was; she had a very interesting answer.

To paraphrase, it went something like this: You have to have great staying power to be in this business and you have to be able to absorb mistakes and take risks. If you are good at this, and careful, you can buy 10 homes at auction and flip them: You'll lose your shirt on two of them, you'll make some decent money on six of them, and you'll make an absolute killing on the other two.

The bottom line is buying a home from a bank or especially a foreclosure on the courthouse steps is not for the faint of heart. I think most people only hear about the two homes where the investor makes a killing and think this is a great way to get rich. If you are going to buy a bank-owned property to resell, make sure you have the knowledge and experience so you know exactly what you are getting into. Don't believe everything you hear and remember that reality TV is designed as entertainment and not reality.

THE RETIRED ENGINEER HOUSE

Retired engineer houses are some of my favorite homes. Sometimes I receive a three-page long, single-spaced disclosure statement explaining how, back in 1984, a hairline crack was noted at the NW corner and was sealed with three applications of epoxy resin.

I Have Seen

- Notes that explained how the hot water heaters had been drained and cleaned annually
- Diagrams of how the irrigation systems and drainage systems work
- Detailed disclosure statements
- Blueprints
- Well organized files showing receipts and permits for work
- Photographs of additions, repairs, or remodel work performed

Little Things I Love

- The wrench hanging off the gas meter to shut the gas off in an emergency
- The sign that indicates the location of the main water shut off
- The compulsively organized shelving and well cared for tools in the garage
- The kitchen pantry where all of the food items are organized on labeled shelves
- Finding anything done with a label maker—that's a great sign that the home has been well maintained. Think about it—anyone so obsessed with organization that they use a label maker will not tolerate a leaking roof

- The service stickers on the furnace that show annual furnace servicing

Beware of Needs for Updates

One thing to beware of in these homes is that there is a big difference between a *well maintained home* and an *updated home.* Sometimes in these homes you find water heaters from when Jimmy Carter was president. While it is amazing that they still work, you should not be surprised if systems like this do not continue to work when a new occupant moves in. These homes can make for a tricky inspection when everything is working. A good inspection can help you understand how old the disposable systems are and if they are past their reliable design life.

THE BUSY FAMILY HOUSE

These are usually pretty straightforward. Many of these homes require extensive disposable system repair and replacement. Why? The parents were so busy getting their kids to school and soccer practices, making the meals, and then getting themselves off to work that they really did not have time to keep up their house.

While the repair and replace list can be long on these types of homes, they tend to be houses where people are not trying to cover things up. Expect the need for new paint, carpet, appliances, furnaces, and water heater—all disposable systems.

Beware of Buying if not Part of a Busy Family

Busy family homes are not well suited to the retired engineer type of buyer. It can be difficult and even expensive to fully repair some of the damage to these homes. If you are looking for something closer to perfection, this is not the home for you.

For example, expect dings and nicks on walls, floors, millwork, and cabinets. Some of these can be difficult to really fix in a cost-effective way. Often cosmetic repairs on these homes are put off until a more extensive renovation project is executed. These types of homes are usually better suited to a new family that wants to come in and clean up some disposable systems and is willing to live with some nicks and dings.

THE RENTAL

Many people who own rental properties have this goal: To cash out the value of the house by collecting as much rent as possible and limit their expenses as much as possible. As a result, it is typical for the rental to have systems well past their reliable design lives. Rentals can often be major fixers. For example, take a property that has been rented for 20 years; it is now hitting the 15 to 20 year maintenance cycle of any house. Combine that with deferred maintenance and little care for the building, and there could be some serious dollars needed to update this home. While some rental homes are better than others, you should expect the need for extensive updates and repairs.

NEW CONSTRUCTION

New construction has an interesting reputation. On one hand, there is a sense that new houses are cheaply built: Poor quality materials, poor workmanship, and poor design, all being thrown together as quickly as possible. New construction has become an icon of our disposable and profit-driven society.

On the other hand, it's unfair to compare today's houses with our older houses: Old growth lumber scarcely exists and oil is no longer $2 a barrel. If we are going to continue to build houses, we must find new materials and learn to build homes that require less energy to operate. In addition, some of our systems like foundations and wiring are far superior to our older homes. It becomes difficult to make accurate comparisons.

My take on new construction is that the quality of new construction isn't significantly better or worse than old construction. Most homes that are not built well are that way because people could not afford to build them well. Our old homes that were poorly built are more forgiving because they have great dry potential, coupled with old growth lumber, so they are less likely to rot. But many of the poorly built old homes have been torn down. We can marvel at the ones that have survived but the reality is that time has culled out the good ones for us to admire.

When I think about new construction, I like to break it down into three primary categories.

1. **The custom home.** Often these are not even inspected after construction. The homeowner has paid architects and builders to build this home and they do not feel as though a home inspection is needed. When well executed, these are often beautiful and well built homes. But be cautious with extreme designs: Unique homes are unique problems no matter how much money was spent building it. Some eccentric house designs are vulnerable to failure and high-maintenance, and they are difficult to execute

well. Keep in mind that The National Park Service struggles to maintain a few of Frank Lloyd Wright's homes. Exposed rooftop decks are a great example of a risky design common to fancy custom homes.

2. **The one-off or "spec house."** A notch below the custom home, these are typically a canned house; a set of plans that was purchased by a builder and put onto a lot. These are home designs that were not necessarily planned to fit on the lot—it's more like the house just landed in that spot. You need to be careful of these. Some of these are fantastic but look for signs of amateur workmanship that make you wonder how many of these this builder has done.

3. **The development.** Developments can be high-end or cost-per-foot conscious. Either way, developments typically involve a larger builder with just a handful of plans pounding out roughly the same house multiple times. Problems in developments are often the same on every house: the roofs are getting old, the siding is a bad product, the plumber did lousy work because he was going through a divorce, the drainage is done poorly. It is often hard to predict these things when they are new. Many of the now-recalled products being used in the 1990s were not recalled when they were installed. Builders thought they were doing the right thing at the time.

What to Look For

The hardest part about new construction is that the home has not been lived in. It is easier to inspect a home that has been out in the weather for 5 to 10 years and has had the toilets flushed 500 times because you can see what worked and what failed. My rule of thumb is that after 5 years you really find out if there were some weak links in the design or execution of a new building, especially as relates to plumbing, drainage, and the exterior envelope.

What I look for during new construction inspections is the type of list I am putting together. My hope is that the list reads like a punch list of incomplete items. I worry when I start finding signs of amateur workmanship that make me lose confidence in the builder. A few areas I feel least confident about are plumbing, drainage, and the exterior envelope because these are difficult to really "see" in a finished house during a visual inspection.

Please note that most if not all states require some amount of a builder warranty on new construction. If you are buying new construction, I recommend consulting with your attorney or Realtor about the warranty provided by builders in your state.

THE ARTIST'S HOUSE

My father and mother were artists—they were filmmakers. They loved houses and took great pride in the physical appearance of the inside of their houses. This emphasized the color of the walls, the art hanging on the walls, and the vibe of an historic and unique house that was not cookie-cutter. They always seemed particularly keen on having a great dining room in which to throw dinner parties.

On one memorable occasion when I was a boy, we were invited to dinner at the home of a business associate of my father. This business associate lived in a gorgeous historic home that was so well cared for it just glistened at every turn. This was the retired engineer's house. The paint was flawless. The roof didn't even have a leaf on it. The lawn was manicured. You could eat off the bathroom floors they were so clean. My family and I tiptoed around the dinner party mildly terrified that we might accidentally upend a drink and cause an unimaginable stir.

In the car driving home after the party, we were riding in silence when my father exclaimed, "Well, I could live in that house for 30 years and never need to fix a thing!"

My mother and I roared with laughter since our own house seemed to be held together by duct tape, but his point emphasizes exactly what some owners want from a house: to simply live in it and throw dinner parties. There is not a thing wrong with this, but after 10 to 20 years of this type of ownership, you should expect the need for a round of new love to be applied to the artist's house, especially to those systems that do not provide a more immediate cosmetic gratification.

Our artist's house needed an exterior paint job and a new roof and we had put off repairs to an exterior staircase that was going to need to be rebuilt soon. My dad just kept putting off important maintenance because there were other things he would rather do with his limited time and money.

THE REALITY TV HOUSE

The reality TV house is probably the saddest category of house on this list. I developed this category in the wake of the 2008 housing bubble and crash. As the wave of foreclosures hit my community, I began to see a surprising number of houses that were in the middle of arrestingly extensive and illogical remodel projects. Kitchens half torn apart with granite slabs poorly installed and laminate flooring laid in haste with large gaps wherever the installer came to a place that might require the use of a measuring tape. I began to wonder if all of these TV shows boasting of the great profits to be made by renovating and flipping homes were misleading people into taking on projects that were a bit out of their league.

This category of house is similar to a poorly executed flipped house. You need to try and understand the scope of what was touched. These homes are characterized by people working on the house doing things that they had no experience doing because they saw it done on TV. You can expect the need to "strip back" much of the work done to these homes before you can finish the house properly.

THE BUILDER'S HOUSE

The builder's house can be one of the best houses that you will see, or they can go the other way and resemble a poorly done flipped house. Your goal is to try and see how meticulous the owner was and if they approached the work done to the house in a cosmetic way or a deep systems way.

Put yourself in the place of a builder: Builders are busy and they spend all day building houses for other people. Then they come home and work on their own house. They may not spend as much time working on their own home as they would like. Perhaps they even leave some things incomplete, thinking, *I can finish that later.* While this is true, the problem is that sometimes later never comes. Some builder's homes can have a long list of odds-and-ends repairs that are needed when "later" arrives at home inspection time. For a good builder's house, the builder/ owner seems to be slightly obsessive-compulsive. The builders/owners are craftsmen who pour time, love, and skill into their home. These are gems. You love buying a home from one of these builders because, although everything may not be completed, the materials and the finishes are often first rate.

CONCLUSION

I hope this gives you some good ideas on how you can use the type of owner of a house to help you define what kind of house you are buying and what type of maintenance you are likely to find. When combined with sorting homes by age, and your newfound knowledge of house systems, you are starting to develop keen skills for looking at houses.

SORTING HOMES BY TYPE **11**

One of the fun things about spending more than a decade inspecting thousands of homes is watching patterns emerge from the different types of homes you inspect. If you can understand how to sort homes by "type," it will enhance your ability to see and understand the houses you are looking at. The goal is that with some practice, you will start to combine house "types" with some of the other house-sorting skills we are learning (such as owners and age and architectural styles) and your house descriptions will come alive. Armed with this new vocabulary, you might say something like, "yeah, that is a mid-century modern good grandma house," or, "that's a turn-of-the-century neighborhood fixer with a bad foundation," and that sequence of 10 or so words will actually tell you an extraordinary amount about the house.

In this chapter, homes are broken into several general "types" that I see daily. Other types exist and you may start to devise types that are endemic to your community. Once you are able to determine the type of home you are looking at, you will be better prepared to compartmentalize some of the issues you are likely to encounter.

The types of homes discussed here include the cabin/cottage construction, The quirky house, the one-off, the neighborhood house, the cul-de-sac house, the McMansion, the mansion, the fixer, the tear down, the blocker, the condo, the townhouse, and the manufactured home versus the mobile home.

THE CABIN/COTTAGE CONSTRUCTION

I have a bias to confess: I love cabins. I have lived in cabins and I would have no problem buying and living in another humble old cabin on a beautiful lot. One thing to keep in mind when buying a cabin is that there is a good chance that most of the value of what you are buying is in the land. A useful exercise to employ with cabins is trying to determine what the land is worth and what the house is worth. Answering these questions will help orient your expectations for the "built" part of your real estate purchase.

Cabin Story

I once inspected an adorable cabin for an older couple who were entering retirement. The cabin was on a beautiful piece of land and was surrounded with amazing landscaping, including gardens with blooming perennials and annual flowers. The outside of the cabin had well painted clapboard siding and an adorable roofline. Inside glowed with beautifully painted bead-board ceilings and it featured a gourmet $100,000 kitchen. It was quaint, charming, and gorgeous.

Guess what? I didn't like it. What bothered me most was that as I started to look at the bones of the cabin, they were in a state that made it nearly a tear down: it had a post and pier foundation that was failing in places, damage to the frame from wood destroying organisms, extensive settlement, old pipes, old wiring, and a pervasive and disgusting rodent problem. The house that I saw looked absolutely nothing like the house that was apparent on the surface. What you see is *not* what you get. It fell to me to try and show my clients the harder-to-see parts of the building that was at the core of what they were buying with the "built" part of this particular investment.

The bottom line is that if a home has a cabin-like foundation and frame, it really is not a good candidate to make it a fancy home unless you do commensurate updates to the old core and entrenched systems. Homes like this should generally be maintained on an as-needed basis until they are torn down or extensively rebuilt. Finishes are best kept commensurate with the building. So if the home you are looking for is a cabin, make sure you have the correct expectations for this type of structure.

THE QUIRKY HOUSE

I have another bias: I like quirky houses. I live in a quirky house that I have added onto and contributed, in my own small way, to its quirkiness.

Quirky houses are those that began as one roofline and floor plan and are now a different roofline and floor plan due to renovations and additions.

A good quirky house can help you break out of the cookie-cutter home without the associated cost of a custom, architecturally designed house. Good quirky houses have rooflines and floor plans that work and show a logical progression and execution to the work that has been performed. Good quirky homes, like any good remodeled home, often include permits, receipts for work, and even blueprints.

Bad quirky houses are another matter. They are so strange that the normal defining characteristics of architectural style have disappeared and the house is now a mishmash. Bad quirky houses have dysfunctional rooflines, illogical floor plans, and poorly executed workmanship. These are houses to be wary of. These are one of the types of homes that, at the end of an inspection, leave me wondering, *what else do I not know about this building? What is hiding behind those walls?*

THE ONE-OFF

My business mentor once said to me, "unique homes are unique problems." Truer words have seldom been spoken. The one-off house is a house that is unique—there are no other houses like it. If architecturally designed and custom built by a good builder, the one-off can be a fantastic house, but it can also lead to complicated problems.

One-off houses that are brand new and have advanced and unique designs are not to be trusted. We simply do not know how they will perform. Look at the exterior envelope design and see if it is conservative or aggressive. Even well built houses with exposed designs can fail. Think complicated rooflines, rooftop decks, exposed turrets, lots of exposed glass, and southwest facing in-swing French doors—all high risk and high-maintenance designs. These types of houses are not necessarily bad houses, but they might require the support of a big check to fix or maintain. These are generally not well suited to you if you are a conservative, risk-intolerant buyer.

THE NEIGHBORHOOD HOUSE

The neighborhood house is what you often see in a city or suburb where a whole series of grid-like streets are built at the same time. I think of these not as cul-de-sac neighborhoods but those older, mature neighborhoods, with grand tree-lined streets. Many of these developments were built in the 1900s through the 1950s. These homes are often sound and reliable real estate investments where what you see is what you get. The condition of these houses is likely a reflection of the relative wealth and prosperity of the neighborhood at the present time. Wealthy neighborhood houses are often well maintained. Run-down neighborhood houses are often run-down. The same is true for the quality of the original build: well built neighborhood homes are more likely found in neighborhoods that were wealthy when the home was built.

THE CUL-DE-SAC HOUSE

Cul-de-sac homes can be safe and reliable. This type of construction implies homes that are built in the suburbs, usually on curving dead-end or looping streets that are not on a grid system. Though versions of cul-de-sacs are an ancient planning concept, they really took off in America starting around the 1960s.

The advantage to building cul-de-sac homes is that builders often worked out the bugs of a few designs and then repeated the homes over and over. Also, homes sited this way often have more privacy and more yard than their grid-tied neighborhood counterparts. On the downside, this can lead to a cookie-cutter neighborhood where all the homes look similar.

As a general rule, the older the cul-de-sac neighborhood, the larger the backyard. The newest versions of this concept seem to have postage stamp yards while the older versions can be quite spacious.

One drawback to production oriented construction is that if there is a flaw in the construction—such as bad siding—then the entire neighborhood will suffer from the same problem. This type of construction does not ensure perfect, well built homes, but it does tend to produce straightforward homes with more predictability when it comes to repair and maintenance.

Tip: Look and ask around. You can often learn a lot about a cul-de-sac house and its associated benefits and problems by talking to the neighbors or even looking at the neighbors' homes.

For example, when you drive into one of these neighborhoods, look at the roofs. If you see some brand new looking roofs and some really old-looking roofs you can quickly wonder which state the roof on your prospective house is in and make an educated guess as to how much useful life remains on the roof. What else do you see in the neighboring homes? New siding? Maybe there is a recalled siding product? Ask yourself, "Are the homes nearby well maintained or are they poorly maintained homes that are more likely rentals?" "Are the yards kept up or overgrown by weeds?" These questions will help you learn a lot about the cul-de-sac home you are considering before you even show up to the house.

THE McMANSION

These are large houses, usually on large suburban lots on cul-de-sac streets. These houses are often similar to the cul-de-sac houses, but someone has hit the "giganto" button and installed higher-end finishes. These homes can often have a surprisingly inexpensive cost per square foot because of the efficiencies of building so large—the cost per foot generally goes down the larger you build. I call some of these homes "acres of sheetrock."

Expect higher maintenance costs simply because of the size of these homes. A new roof or a paint job in these houses can be surprisingly expensive. Also, look to see how exposed the envelope is. These larger homes can have more exposed envelopes, which can lead to high exterior maintenance costs. Like most homes of this ilk, I worry less about structure and wiring and more about water problems associated with envelope repair and drainage.

THE MANSION

Mansions reflect solid well built homes and are usually sound investments. I think of mansions as old grand homes in established neighborhoods. Mansions can have some expensive price tags hanging over them for both maintenance and repair due to their size, age, and the quality of their finishes. For example, if a mansion has gorgeous old leaded glass wood windows that are failing on the exposed faces of the building,

you are not exactly going to replace them with the least-expensive white vinyl windows now, are you? Expect maintenance to be expensive and custom and require local craftsmen. Restoring an old mansion would be a fun and gratifying experience but one I am unlikely to ever have. These types of homes require serious checkbooks to buy, update, and maintain.

THE FIXER

The fixer can be subjective. It is important to keep in mind that many fixers are often being lived in quite happily by current owners. The current owner may have learned to live with old and unreliable finishes and systems that sometimes fail. That noted, when a house like this has a change in the occupant, then what the building needs is also likely to change.

The Cosmetic Fixer

If you watched a cable TV home channel, you've seen this type of fixer. This is the one that TV programs showcase when they boast about how easy and great it is to flip houses. The problem is that perfect cosmetic fixers are difficult to find.

The Spreadsheet Fixer

The spreadsheet fixer is a house that needs a fair amount of disposable and even entrenched systems work, as well as cosmetic updates. With this home, the repair risk appears to be low because the updates that are needed are fairly predictable as to where they begin and end. Expect to update disposable systems as well as some limited entrenched systems, but overall the bones should be good. These are exemplified by the "good grandma house," and can be fantastic project houses.

The Disaster Fixer

If you've watched the movie *The Money Pit*, you know the stereotype. The disaster fixer is characterized by chronic dysfunction in core house systems. Sometimes people ignore this and try to apply cosmetic repairs to these homes, leaving the chronic dysfunction with core systems unresolved. The disaster fixer is the textbook example of lipstick on a pig. The worst disaster fixers creep into a different type of house altogether—the tear down. One concept I worry about on these is "the peeled onion"; you start by fixing a piece of siding and it leads to the window above, framing behind, the sill plate, rim joist, and roof and gutter. The next thing you know, you've torn half the house apart and imploded your budget.

THE TEAR DOWN

Sadly, the cost to repair a building can sometimes exceed its value. At this point the house is a tear down. It is subjective at what point a building becomes a tear down. I have seen very nice homes torn down because the value of the lot on which they were built has so outstripped the value of the house that they are simply removed. This is common in areas where waterfront land has become extremely valuable.

The guiding principle at work on other tear-down homes is that the cost per foot for remodel work is generally much more expensive than building new. This is because there is a relative efficiency to building new that is lost when you are tearing into old things to make repairs. Experienced builders in your community should be able to help you make these analyses to see if a house is worth repairing or renovating. You can also take the skills gained from this book about core and entrenched systems and apply this analysis to the house. What part of these systems is worth keeping and what needs replacing? If too many core systems are in need of replacement, the justification for renovation becomes increasingly difficult.

THE "BLOCKER"

"Blocker" or block homes are built entirely from CMU, concrete masonry units—also called concrete blocks or masonry blocks. These homes tend to have slab on grade foundations and are simple one-story homes often built after World War II.

Block homes are at risk from water condensation problems. They usually have either poor or no mechanical ventilation systems to move interior air. This can lead to high relative humidity. If the walls are not well insulated, they can be cold in the winter, which creates a perfect condensing surface and seasonal condensation problems—think mold.

If these homes have old piping or wiring systems, they can be difficult to update. There is no crawl space if they are slab on grade and they often have tight attic spaces. Expect these homes to be of marginal quality, but affordable.

The good news is because they are all masonry construction, they do not tend to have extensive rot problems. One more advantage is that there is an underlying simplicity to these houses—and by now you know that simple is good.

THE CONDO

Let's think of condominiums in two pieces: There is one piece you control, which is typically from the walls of the unit in. Then there is the rest of the building, from the walls of the unit out, that your condo association controls.

Inside

The inside of a condo unit is generally straightforward and that means there are rarely too many large surprises. There may be items to repair, but these tend to be more obvious repairs to disposable systems, such as installing a new water heater, making updates to kitchens and bathrooms, or replacing old, stained carpet.

The exception is when you find an unsafe or recalled entrenched or core system. An example is single-strand aluminum wiring or a recalled or failing plumbing product that you suspect runs throughout the building. This is a big red flag because you may be able to fix your unit, but if your neighbor does not fix their unit, a resulting house fire or plumbing leak could quickly become your problem. This reminds me of a beer cozy I once saw that read, "My attitude is your problem."

The outside of a condominium in the first stages of being wrapped in preparation to repair the exterior envelope.

Outside

The outside of a condominium is where you will typically find the most risk. While it is true that you are not personally responsible for this maintenance, if large repairs become needed to the rest of the building, a portion of the repair could become your financial responsibility.

Every condo has a homeowner association (HOA), which assesses fees for the maintenance and repairs of the common elements of the building. But if the HOA does not have the money to pay for a major repair, then the HOA may need to do what is called a "special assessment." This can be a direct cost to you and some special assessments can cost tens of thousands of dollars.

For this reason, if you are inspecting a condominium, be sure to ask your home inspector to look at the whole building. This is not a "commercial inspection," but it should include a look around the outside of the building, the roof, and the parking garage below. A cursory look at the building's common elements will help you better understand if the HOA is on a healthy path for maintenance or if they are lagging behind.

Important Condo Vocabulary

Condominiums have some unique terminology that you should be familiar with if you are buying a condo:

- **Exterior Envelope:** This refers to the exterior skin of the building. This term is used on large exposed buildings, since you cannot treat siding, decks, doors, windows, and the roof as separate systems. All of these systems tie together and failures in an envelope tend to occur where one or more of these systems come together. Envelope repairs can be very expensive.

- **Envelope Study:** Envelope studies are performed by engineering firms that specialize in evaluating the exterior skins of buildings. Ask the HOA if such a study has been done. While some of these studies may not be very detailed or helpful, some are and even include valuable color photos and "destructive testing." This is where limited sections of the building are torn open to investigate if the building is staying dry.

- **Wrapped:** This is a term used to describe a building that has had an envelope problem and has been wrapped in scaffolding and a large plastic barrier while the repair work gets done. Look around as you drive through a city and you may see an existing building that is currently "wrapped," and under envelope repair.

- **Reserve Study or Cost Analysis:** Ideally, a qualified contractor or engineer has executed the reserve study. This study will project out the costs for building maintenance, including keeping up the landscaping, replacing the roof, servicing the elevators, etc. The study should include a detailed budget, based on the proposed building maintenance. Some reserve studies seem detailed and well thought out, others seem to be a bit more of a "dartboard science."

- **Reserves:** This is the amount of money the HOA has saved from its dues.

- **Special Assessment:** Remember, the HOA is not a wealthy benefactor for the condo. The only asset most HOAs have is the savings from collecting monthly dues. The assets within the building are owned by the individual owners, so if the building needs new siding and new windows and has no money, guess who has to pay?

Condo Tip 1

Look for condos that have been out in the weather for 5 years or more. It is difficult to know how a new building will perform. Construction defect litigation in condo construction is very common. This is where the HOA ends up suing the developer for construction defects discovered after the build. Once the building has been out in the weather for 5 years or more, the odds of defects suddenly coming up seems to go down.

Condo Tip 2

Beware of old buildings that have been recently converted from apartments to condos. States may not require that all of the building's systems be updated. The result is that you may end up with a new condo HOA that has no money and a building maintenance liability.

Condo Tip 3

Sometimes finding a condo that has been recently "wrapped" or extensively repaired can be good. This type of extensive repair work often follows litigation with a developer and the new work has often been extensively engineered and checked and may be of much better quality than the original construction. The hope is that the original building flaws were discovered and repaired and now the building is on a sound path for lower maintenance.

Condo Tip 4

When thinking about condominiums, try identifying a "personality" to the HOA. Is this an HOA that is run by retired real estate developers, attorneys, and engineers? Or, is the HOA comprised of very old members who have no interest in maintaining the building? You want to see if there is a logical game plan for assessing dues and implementing maintenance and repairs.

Condo Tip 5

Condos with more than two bedrooms can be difficult to find.

THE TOWNHOUSE

The townhouse is an historic type of construction. Our East Coast cities have plenty of old, regal townhouses—think brownstones in Manhattan.

In recent years, the modern townhouse is making resurgence. In cities like Seattle, where there is little room to build new housing, old homes are being torn down and townhouses are being built in their place. This is because builders can fit four or more units onto a lot that once had just one house.

The downside of some townhouse designs is that you may share a wall with your neighbor, so expect less privacy and less yard or outdoor space. You also may share a roof and even siding and decks with your neighbor. If the townhouse is new, this should not be much of an issue for the first 10 to 20 years. However, once roofs start needing replacement and siding needs paint, it sometimes is unclear how this type of maintenance will be performed. Make sure there is a maintenance agreement in place.

With no maintenance agreement, half-painted townhomes are a common occurrence. In this case, the owner of the right side of the house painted and the owner of the left side of the house left the existing failing paint.

THE MANUFACTURED HOME VERSUS THE MOBILE HOME

I find that this distinction is not well understood in the real estate world, even by experienced real estate agents and some appraisers. Let's see how they differ.

Mobile Homes

Mobile homes generally do not have foundations. They are often resting on masonry blocks with a metal strapping system below them that ties them to some type of footing system. Mobile homes usually have a vapor barrier below the wood framing and metal axles attached to the bottom from when they were wheeled into place.

Mobile homes generally have short useful service lives.

You should think of mobile homes as disposable houses and depreciating assets. The average life span is 35 to 40 years, at which point the cost to repair may exceed the cost to replace. That is a problem when it comes to fixing up old mobile homes—you bump up against fairly inexpensive replacement costs compared to repair costs.

Mobile homes are built to be very tight, and that means they have little in the way of natural make-up air. To compensate, they use fan systems. Unfortunately these systems are often loud, broken, or disabled and may not perform well. Finally, many of the building materials in mobile homes are low-end and can contain high levels of toxic materials, such as formaldehyde. In short, indoor air quality is suspect in these homes.

Manufactured Homes

The history of prefabricated houses goes very far back: In 1906, Sears, Roebuck & Co. offered a pre-fabricated house in its catalog.

Manufactured homes are generally stick-built off site and trucked in and placed onto a foundation. These homes can sometimes be difficult to distinguish from regular stick-built homes, depending on how well they were made.

There are some manufactured home companies that assemble custom houses in panels and truck them in for comparatively quick on-site assembly. If you think about it, it makes some sense to build all the wood frame of a house in a shop where the wood stays dry and can be cut more precisely. This can cut down on on-site construction time and construction waste, and it reduces the time the wood is in the weather.

Not all manufactured homes are well built or well maintained, but a good one on a good foundation can result in a quality house.

OVERVIEW

Learning to think critically about the types of houses you are looking at will help align your expectations for maintenance, repairs, and updates. It should also help inform your house search to better weed out the types of homes that are not likely to suit your desires. When combined with some of the technical background and the other sorting strategies outlined here, you should find yourself becoming a more sophisticated homebuyer.

SORTING HOMES BY ARCHITECTURAL STYLE 12

From early cave dwelling to the modern high rise, there is an extraordinary breadth of residential architecture in which humans have dwelled. Whatever type of structure you want to make your next home, you are certain to be choosing from only a small sliver of this diversity.

It's important to understand what part of that sliver is regionally specific to the area where you are shopping for a house. You need to familiarize yourself with the styles of structures that have been built in your community:

- What are the styles of homes within your price range?
- What decades did the architectural style tend to be built in?
- What are the relative strengths and weaknesses of the styles you are considering?
- What are the typical materials used in constructing these buildings?

CLIMATE AND CULTURAL INFLUENCE STRUCTURE

The architectural designs and styles of each community reflect the economic and social history of that community as well as the regional climate and availability of local building materials. For example, you are not likely to find Creole Cottage architecture in the mountains of Colorado and there is a good reason for that—the style is not suited to the climate and the heavy mountain snow could collapse the roof. You will not find many Cape Cod homes in the southwestern United States and if you did the traditional clapboard wood siding would deteriorate quickly under the punishing desert sun.

The styles of buildings intrinsic to a community are often the designs best suited to that area. In the Seattle area for example, I am suspicious of architecture that looks as though it migrated here from Santa Fe or Los Angeles. While I appreciate the architecture of flat roofs and admire the light that comes into a home when it has no roof overhangs, these designs can be a recipe for failure when the design is taken from a hot, dry, desert climate and moved to a wet, cold climate.

Your own style is another important factor when thinking of houses. If you want a house with a strong architectural point of view, you may also want furniture that matches. This can become a lifestyle. I have done inspections for clients who are moving from a cute craftsman bungalow to a beautiful mid-century modern and I hear them bemoan the fact that they will need all new furniture and art. Clearly a first-world problem, but a consideration nonetheless since the style of house you buy can dictate the way you live and the furniture and art you own.

Maintenance and updates are also influenced by style. Homes with a strong architectural point of view can be more complicated to repair and renovate; you can't just go to Home Depot and pick any old thing off the shelf to update these houses. Repairs and updates on "interesting" homes can more closely resemble "restoration" than "repair." This can be fun and rewarding but it's more like owning a fine collectors car than a Honda Accord.

Home renovations should also be guided by a background understanding of architectural style if you want to renovate homes with class, flair, and logic. You can always spot a house where background knowledge and acknowledgement of architectural style was lacking, even without being an expert. Homes like this lack continuity and have a mishmash of styles that even the untrained eye can pick up.

If you are unfamiliar with general architectural styles, I recommend spending a bit of time on the web. The Internet offers a treasure trove of architectural images to help you discern the different styles. Wikipedia, for example, has reference pages with dozens of architectural styles for you to compare and contrast.

Below are a few examples of common architectural styles that I run into frequently. My comments are intended to help you see how certain styles of homes have specific design characteristics, which you may or may not like. Once you start to recognize some of these trends, it will provide you with another tool to help "see" the houses you are looking at.

Please distinguish my comments from a true architecture study. The observations below are based on my personal experience and they are more practical and much less detailed and convoluted than some of the true architectural analyses I have read. They are intended to provoke your own thoughts of how you can look at and break down houses like a home inspector. These comments may parallel breakdown by age; this is because architectural styles change with the times and are frequently associated with a specific decade or two. While these descriptions and experiences are regionally specific, many of these generalizations will hold true for much of the architecture in the country.

THE FOUR SQUARE

Often built in the late 1800s to 1930s, this was a simple boxy style of house. I think of them as **Victorian** style houses that have been simplified. They are often two and a half stories tall with four large box-like rooms per floor. They have large front porches and an entry door right in the middle of the house in the middle of the front porch. Don't expect master suites unless they have been updated—usually one bathroom per floor if you're lucky. The four square are generally larger homes with a box-like appearance. Upscale versions of these houses will be dressed up with

elegant craftsman details like intricate braces under the eaves. Simple versions of these homes are essentially large boxes with simple hip rooflines.

The floor plans in these homes are similar. The main floor consists of an entry area off the front door with a hallway leading back to a stairway down to the basement and a large square kitchen—sometimes there is even a small powder bathroom here. On the opposite side of the main floor are two large box rooms—a dining room and a living room with a fireplace. The stairs are often large and comfortable by old-house standards. Expect four bedrooms and a bathroom on the second floor. Some of these homes have stairs to a half story above and others have attic hatches that access a large attic space.

CRAFTSMAN/BUNGALOW

These can be beautiful homes, often built in the turn of the century through the 1920s. Do not expect big open floor plans—these homes are typically boxy on the inside because all the framing needs to land on top of other framing below. Expect big front porches and substantial roof overhangs supported by braces. The rooflines are often simple gables with sensible pitches such as $5/_{12}$ and maybe one or two simple dormers. Many of these homes have sagging front porches and sagging roof overhangs—a relic from under-framing done in this era. The floor plans tend to be

Photo courtesy of Frank Jenkins.

traditional with formal dining and living rooms. Updated versions may have large kitchens but these may have been added onto—original versions of these homes can have small and basic kitchen spaces. Don't expect master suites—usually one bathroom upstairs and one downstairs unless additions have been made. The stair systems in these homes are hit or miss—the stately versions have nice stairs and the more humble versions have steep marginal stairs. Look for neat craftsmen details inside such as impressive millwork in dining and living rooms, leaded glass or stained glass windows, and handmade tiles around the fireplace.

Bungalow Knockoff

I once inspected a new construction house in a neighborhood where they were knocking off old bungalow style houses. This house had the large roof overhangs characteristic of the old bungalows and when I looked closely I could see the eaves on this brand new house were sagging. They did too good of a job copying the old ones.

TUDOR

These houses have steep roof pitches, brick siding at least on the front of the house, and leaded glass windows. Some nice specimens have beautiful solid wood front doors, often with a curved arch. Inside you can find coved living room ceilings done in lath and plaster and trim and

Tudors sometimes have stucco siding with wood trim laid into the siding, as shown here. Photo courtesy of Frank Jenkins.

windows made from mahogany. Hardwood floors are common on the main floor and may have inlay. Expect small boxy rooms and not big open floor plans. Expect small kitchens unless additions have been made. These homes often have steep treacherous stair systems. The second floor is often a half story with some vaulted sections of ceiling and knee walls forming small attic spaces behind short walls. Like most old homes, don't expect a master suite unless one has been added.

CAPE COD

I find it difficult to peg down this style of house because any time I see a house that lacks a strong architectural point of view it seems to be called a Cape Cod. I see Cape Cod homes from lots of different eras: 1920s, 1950s, and 1980s are examples I can most readily point to. The essence of the Cape Cod style is simple homes that lack fancy details with simple steep gable rooflines originally designed to shed winter snows. These homes are often a story and a half, and if there is finished space on the second floor, expect those short knee walls and low vaulted ceiling. Also on the second floor, expect marginal steep or narrow stairs, especially in the older ones. Window shutters originated in New England to fend off the blustery coastal winter storms and the look of window shutters is still alive on Cape Cod homes, often done today with faux plastic shutters as

Photo courtesy of Frank Jenkins.

a tribute to this once functional design. Siding is traditionally clapboard and windows were originally done with split glass windows.

Economic History

In the 1700s in America when Cape Cod style homes were being built, the glass for windows was imported from England and was a premium product. New Englanders started using a collection of small 6 × 8 inch glass panes to make larger windows as the small panes of glass were easier and more reliably transported across the Atlantic. This is the birth of the split glass window that we think of as having so much character today.

MID-CENTURY MODERN

The best versions of the mid-century modern house have surprisingly contemporary floor plans and designs considering they are now often 55 to 65 years old. Many of the best versions from this era are custom so the insides are not as predictable as some of the other styles. The emphasis of mid-century modern was to open spaces up and bring futuristic designs to the otherwise boxy world of houses prior to the 1950s. Expect extensive and interesting use of glass in large open walls to bring the outside in. Look for interesting lighting, built-ins, and furniture that often go with this style.

SPLIT-LEVEL

The split-level is the classic blue collar 1970s family house. Many of these are on first-generation cul-de-sac developments. The best specimens of these homes are great family homes due to their simple design—remember this guiding principle: simplicity is your friend. The floor plans can vary a little but there are often three bedrooms and two bathrooms and a semi-open kitchen, dining, and living room on the main floor. Expect relatively small rooms though some fancier versions have decent sized rooms. The entry to the house is usually on a mid-level landing in the middle of the house—you head up to the living room or down into the basement from the landing. Expect a basement to be half bonus room and half garage with a small bathroom and laundry room. These usually have modern poured concrete foundations, simple gable rooflines and modern wiring. Watch for old and poorly cared-for systems. Check for moisture in the basement. If it's the early 1970s, check for single-strand aluminum wiring. These homes tend to be: what you see is what you get.

A-FRAME

The A-frame is the quintessential ski cabin/mountain house. The steep roof pitch sheds snow well and is suited to the mountain climate. Many humble versions of these are literally cabins and lack foundations because they are installed on posts and pier blocks. Upscale versions of

the A-frame start transitioning into the prow-style roofline. Lindal Cedar homes are a brand of house characteristic of the prow design with tall two-story walls of windows often taking in a mountain, river, lake, or ocean view. Most of these homes have simple open living rooms, dining rooms, and kitchens. Expect stairs to a loft or bonus space on the second floor. The upscale versions may have basements below, especially if they are a prow-style house built into a hillside.

OVERVIEW

The architectural style of a house is truly one of the bones of a house. Even though it is cosmetic in theory, the style will influence how the house was built and how it will perform—for example, how the roof will shed water and deflect UV rays. The style will also tell you roughly when the home was built, which will influence the building materials used and the type of maintenance and updating you are likely to find. This is not to be overlooked.

Style and design are areas where I find the typical way of sorting homes by system can really break down. I have seen well built houses with nice new systems that have expensive problems where the design and style of the house were not suited to the climate. I sometimes look at complicated rooftop deck systems in my area and think to myself, *Look; an architect designed a water problem.*

There are many more architectural styles of homes than those I have outlined above. The goal here is to give you some tools to learn how to think about how floor plans and features and potential maintenance follow architectural style. Once you become familiar with the styles in your area, it will become an invaluable tool to help you *see* the houses you are looking at. You may even fall in love with a particular style and it can become the signature of your life and your lifestyle.

PART IV

In the Field

GETTING THE MOST FROM YOUR HOME INSPECTION **13**

In addition to learning how to look at homes, it is also valuable to learn how to get the most from your home inspection. Once you understand the inspection process, you can learn to work well with your inspector and be able to read and evaluate your inspection report. Knowing how to do this is crucial to buying the right home.

Let's Explore Some Key Areas

1. Why you should get a home inspected
2. Selecting a home inspector
3. Putting the house in perspective
4. Asking questions without distracting
5. Why your home inspector needs to know your situation
6. Why there are limitations to home inspections
7. What you should be afraid of
8. Knowing the standards of practice

WHY YOU SHOULD GET A HOME INSPECTED

When my wife and I had twin boys, it turned my world upside down. We were both sleep-deprived and stressed and we needed to buy a new house. I found myself having a difficult time making good decisions. Here I am, a professional home inspector realizing that I needed a friend to look at a house for me.

Despite the fact that I had inspected thousands of homes and completed dozens of repairs and remodels, I still needed someone's help. So when I found a house that I wanted to call home, I called my home inspection mentor to come with me and have a look. She kept pointing things out to me that I knew, and I kept saying, "Yeah, yeah, I know that. I can fix that."

Finally she looked at me and said, "Yes you can fix that, but you have two babies and a full-time business. When exactly are you going to find time to fix these things?"

Getting her advice and this third-party point of view was invaluable to me that day. It helped me from making a poor decision. I did not buy that house.

Tip: Read your home inspection report! I was once doing a home inspection and coming off the roof to introduce myself to the prospective homebuyer when we realized, coincidentally, that we were old college friends. He and his wife were buying a fabulous house, but I told them that it needed a new roof, a new master bathroom, and a new water heater. They were thrilled to hear that it was such a great house and they moved in. The roof leaked, the master bathroom leaked, and the water heater died. "Didn't Dylan warn us about all this stuff?" bemoaned my friend's wife. So he went to his computer and downloaded my report, presumably for the first time, and realized that in fact, yes, I had these items in bold red font under Major Concern with photos.

Please read these reports. If they are good reports, we work hard to make them!

SELECTING A HOME INSPECTOR

I would select a home inspector based primarily on their experience and their communications skills—some home inspectors just dump a report on you while others spend a great deal of time on-site working with you to explain to you what they are seeing. Don't underestimate the value of this on-site educational time—it is the most important, in my opinion. You can likely get a clue about their communication skills by going to their website and reading a sample report. I would be suspicious of inspectors who

- Do not have a website
- Do not take photographs
- Use any type of hand-written reporting system
- Use checklist-style reports or reports that do not convey useful information

Tips

- Ask your Realtor and ask your friends and family if they have had a good experience with a local home inspector
- Try finding someone local—local knowledge is valuable
- Try finding someone with at least 5 years of experience
- Check their website and read their sample reports
- Look for membership in professional organizations such as ASHI and InterNACHI
- Online reviews can be helpful but also misleading. An inspector may have thousands of satisfied clients who did not take the time to write a flattering review while one bad experience can unfairly smear their reputation. Online reviews are a good indication of the inspector if there are more than 30 or 40 reviews

PUTTING THE HOUSE IN PERSPECTIVE

A good home inspector provides an invaluable service: perspective and context about the house you are proposing to buy. Experienced inspectors have looked at many thousands of houses—this is a perspective that even the best builders and architects are lacking.

Some of my clients ask me to give their house a grade. I find it unfair to grade a house; clearly, a $4 million mansion is nicer than a $50,000 fixer. Better questions to ask your inspector are "How does the house stack up against other homes of similar age and type?" and "Was the list of repairs you found surprising, just what you expected, or better than expected?" This type of context for the discoveries made during an inspection is critical and at the core of what you are paying an experienced home inspector for.

My hope is that the previous chapters in this book will help you have your own context for the discoveries made during a home inspection. That is one of the goals of this book, to help homebuyers have their expectations in better alignment with the houses they are proposing to buy and to help homebuyers better understand the discoveries made during a home inspection.

ASKING QUESTIONS WITHOUT DISTRACTING

I love when my clients are participating in the home inspection—I enjoy having them follow along and ask questions. Not every home inspector likes this, but many do; it gives a sense that you are directly helping your client understand what they are buying.

While this participation can be invaluable to the process, it can become distracting if there are too many questions. Be aware of this fine line. Good questions, observations, and comments can be very helpful. Too many can distract an inspector from their process and lead to a less thorough inspection.

WHY YOUR HOME INSPECTOR NEEDS TO KNOW YOUR SITUATION

In my opinion, a home inspector can help you more when he or she understands your situation. Homes are not purchased without situations. Whether you need more room for a baby, a mother-in-law apartment for an aging parent, an investment property for your retirement, to downsize because the kids are off to college, or your first home, all home purchases come with a situation. Maybe you just got a promotion? A divorce? You are moving from another country? Sharing information about your situation helps a home inspector better understand what they are walking into. Remember, *every house is a great house for the right person at the right price.* So, are you the right person?

I can think of a time recently when I was inspecting a house for my clients, Jane and Preston. As I worked my way through the inspection with them, I got the sense that they did not really want to talk to me about their situation. Preston said they did not want to share with me a prior inspection that was done on the house. They seemed to think that if I came in blind, and had no previous knowledge of the house, the sellers, or their own situation, that I would somehow miraculously come to an unbiased opinion of the house. To me, it felt like I was flying blind.

Let's be honest: There is no such thing as an "unbiased opinion" for *anything*, let alone for houses.

Your home inspector can help you the most if they are prepared. That means sharing with them any prior home inspections, disclosure statements, and knowledge of the seller's situation and helping them to understand you and where you are in your life.

Common Questions that Home Inspectors Could Ask

- Where is this house in your price range?
- Have you made many other offers?

214

- Do you have children, especially young children? Or will young children be visiting often? Think safety concerns.
- Are there many other options you have considered or is this what you found after years of looking?
- Do you have construction experience?
- How much spare time do you have? Are you looking for a project or just a low-maintenance place to live?
- Are there improvement projects with this home that you had in mind?
- Are there relevant disclosures from the seller or any knowledge about the seller that could be useful?
- Do you have any particular concerns? Mold? The roof? The foundation?

Every home inspector is different and some inspectors may not approach the job like this. But in my experience, information is power and sometimes information can make the difference between a good decision and a poor one. Help yourself by sharing information with your inspector; I know that it helps me to help my clients.

WHY THERE ARE LIMITATIONS TO HOME INSPECTIONS— ARE THEY A SCAM?

Let's face this urban myth head-on: There is an uneducated point of view that because home inspectors use pre-inspection agreements, and because home inspections are limited, home inspections are a scam, and your home inspector will likely do a lousy job.

Yes, there are terrible home inspectors who do lousy work. But that is not because the home inspection was a limited visual inspection; it is probably because your home inspector did not do a thorough job, or was not experienced.

Home inspectors must do limited visual inspections, because unlike the ones you may have seen on TV, we cannot rip the walls off the framing to show you what's behind. If we did, we'd be replacing a lot of walls and buying nearly every home we inspected.

For the record, tearing a house apart is called "destructive testing," and occasionally you can hire a specialist to do destructive testing in the middle of a real estate transaction, but as you can imagine, the circumstances and the number of times this actually happens is rare.

Good home inspectors use visual clues and tools such as moisture meters and thermal cameras to look critically at houses. Thoughtful and experienced home inspectors can often find red flags indicating possible hidden problems, which allows you to do additional inspections with a contractor or specialist who can help you understand the full extent of the potential problem. An example might be calling in a roofer to look at the roof and provide an estimate for replacement so you can put a number to a problem. Or, a drainage person might come out and suggest a range of options for repairs so you have a sense of a best-case and worst-case scenario for a more complex drainage problem repair.

A good home inspection is invaluable in helping you make an informed buying decision. If you have had a bad experience with a home inspector in the past, I suggest you do some research before hiring your next inspector. Make sure they are experienced, use professional tools, and write comprehensive reports. Don't just shop around for the least expensive inspection fee—that is a recipe for a poor home inspection. (Refer to the "Selecting a Home Inspector" section above.)

It is important to note that there are virtually no requirements to hire a home inspector; yet, almost everyone pays for a home inspection. The reason? It's a great investment. I can think of times I saved my clients over $60,000 off the purchase price of a house due to needed repairs in exchange for a $600 inspection fee; I bet your stockbroker can't provide a return on investment like that. Home inspections can uncover important and even life-threatening discoveries. Make the investment by hiring a good home inspector.

WHAT YOU SHOULD BE AFRAID OF

One of the real arts to a quality home inspection is evaluating the home to determine how much hidden risk the house presents. By now you know that if a house needs a new roof or a new furnace or a new bathroom, it will be expensive. But you also know that does not make it a bad house. If you decide to rescind your offer to purchase a home because of the roof, furnace, or bathroom, that's fine, because you are making a decision based on data and numbers—an informed decision.

Remember, it's what you don't know that will hurt you. The fact is that *some houses present more barriers to perfect knowledge than others*. I wish this were not true. I wish I could always provide perfect information about every house, but that's simply not possible for most homes.

The goal is for you to know how much risk there may be for you based on what your home inspector sees (and what they are unable to see). This is the tricky and subjective part of home inspections, but it gets at the heart of why you should hire a professional—to help you understand how much risk you are taking on by purchasing the house.

KNOWING THE STANDARDS OF PRACTICE

Frankly, most homebuyers are not going to take the time to read the standards of practice that define a home inspection. If, however, you are the type of person who wants to understand what you are getting into with a home inspection, there is no better place to start than understanding these standards.

The standards of practice define the scope of a home inspection. This is very important. There are a lot of things that are not included in a home inspection and this is because there is so much that one could look at in any given house; you need to define a scope for the inspection so you can define a cost and time frame for the work to be performed. The standards have been created over roughly 40 years in an effort to define a sort of sweet spot: what is the minimum inspection we can do to provide the most information at the least cost? Remember this when you hire a home inspector. You can always pay for additional inspections and more information. Some small examples are well inspections, septic inspections, pest inspections, radon, mold, sewer scopes, infrared, and recalled appliances. This is really about the amount of due diligence you want to do until you are comfortable with the house. Every homebuyer has their own place where they feel comfortable. I have had several clients over the years who hire two separate home inspectors; they want to make sure something does not get missed. If that helps you sleep better at night, then do it.

There is no single standard of practice. States that have licensed home inspectors have their own standards and there are national organizations such as The American Society of Home Inspectors (ASHI) with their standards. The ASHI standards are probably some of the oldest and best in my opinion and I suspect that most states have taken their standards from the ASHI standards[1] to one degree or another.

---

1. See http://getscribeware.com/blog/wp-content/uploads/2015/11/ASHI-Standards-Updated-3-4-2015.pdf.

WOOD DESTROYING ORGANISMS AND OTHER PESTS **14**

Problems with wood destroying organisms (WDOs) should not be taken lightly. They represent a potentially complicated repair to a core system: damage to the wood frame of a building. Extensive problems with WDOs can lead to expensive repairs or make an old house unworthy of renovation if enough of the wood frame is damaged.

WDO problems are regional and site specific. Even in a small geographic area, there can be several different microclimate and soil conditions that create different WDO problems in different areas.

For example, in most of the greater Seattle area, you are unlikely to ever find subterranean termites or extensive anobiid beetle problems. But go southwest of Seattle, to West Seattle, and subterranean termites are common. Now cross the Puget Sound to Kitsap County and you are much more likely to find anobiid beetles than on the east side of the Puget Sound. This is the type of regionally specific information that good home inspectors and pest inspectors learn over time. The bottom line is be sure your home inspector includes a pest inspection as a part of the scope of their work or consider hiring a pest inspector as an additional inspection. In some parts of the country, a pest inspection or termite inspection may even be required to finance the home.

Problems with wood destroying organisms can be scary because the damage done to the building is difficult to see or quantify; this is because damaged wood may be partly or entirely concealed behind finishes. You are also at the mercy of pest control operators and contractors; it can be difficult to distinguish if a scope of service recommended is really necessary or if a contractor could be taking advantage of the situation.

The Two Main Categories of Wood Destroying Organisms

1. WDOs that you can tie to water problems
   - Carpenter ants
   - Dampwood termites
   - Beetles
   - Moisture ants
   - Wood fungus (rot or dry rot)—this is the most common

2. White fungal rot. WDOs that can damage your building even if you do not have a water problem
   - Subterranean termites (left)
   - Formosan termites
   - Carpenter ants (right)

Photo Descriptions

1. Carpenter ants swarming the floor frame below a house
2. Wood "frass" piled up at the base of a floor frame post—frass is the pulp and excrement from wood destroying insects
3. Exit holes and frass from anobiid beetles
4. A pile of moisture ant frass
5. A moisture ant tube—often confused with termite tubes
6. A Moisture ant nest
7. White fungal rot

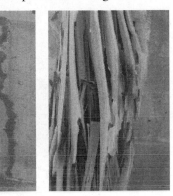

WATER AND WDOs

With the exception of subterranean and Formosan termites, most of our wood destroying organisms are a function of water problems in the building. In many cases, the trick to eliminating wood destroying organisms is diagnosing and eliminating the problematic water source. Sometimes additional treatment may be needed, but often simply drying out the building can stop the wood destroying organisms, allowing damaged wood to be repaired as needed.

While diagnosing water problems can be simple, it is more often complex. For example, if a house has an anobiid beetle problem in wood framing below the house, the crawl space may have inadequate vapor barriers on the earth, inadequate ventilation around the perimeter, and/or seasonal drainage problems. Knowing what it will take to repair the moisture problem may not be completely clear.

One of the most effective strategies for managing water-related wood destroying organisms is to eliminate "conducive conditions" around your property. Understating conducive conditions can help you see and predict wood destroying organism problems when you are touring houses and if you are a homeowner, eliminating these conditions is the organic way you control WDOs in your house. You do not need to be an expert to see these things.

Conducive Conditions to Look For

- Houses in heavily wooded settings
- Wood siding or framing near the ground or in ground contact (pictured top)

This rotted wood and soil up against the house is a conducive condition.

- Rotten stumps or logs around the house (pictured middle)
- Trees and vegetation touching the house (pictured bottom)
- Inadequate or blocked crawl space ventilation—if the house is built with a crawl space configuration—Do you see vents on the side of the house?

- Drainage problems:
  - Downspouts draining adjacent to the foundation
  - Disconnected downspouts
  - Leaking/failing gutters
  - Houses located on a low lot or a boggy, wet lot

TREATING FOR WATER-RELATED WDOs

The organic way to control these water-related WDOs is to eliminate these WDO-conducive conditions, creating a natural barrier around your house. Maintaining your house well to keep building materials dry and eliminate WDO-conducive conditions is the critical first step. Sometimes, this is not enough and chemical treatment may be needed. In my area, carpenter ants and anobiid beetles are the two most common water-related WDOs that require chemical treatment and for this you hire a pest control operator.

THE SINGLE-MOST COMMON WDO: FUNGI

The most common WDO related to water is fungal rot. This is often referred to as dry rot, which is a misnomer, as dry wood does not rot.

Interestingly, it is not the water that rots the wood, but water is required to facilitate the fungus that decays the wood. Wood generally needs at least 20 percent moisture content for wood fungi to develop. So, the way you stop wood rot is to keep wood dry.

When installing wood in outdoor installations, such as below ground posts or exterior decks, it is wise to use wood that is rated for outdoor use. For example, deck structures are often built from pressure-treated lumber—this is wood that has been treated with chemicals to resist fungal decay. The decking might be done in cedar or redwood—species of wood high in tannic acid, which also resist fungal rot even when getting wet.

WDOs NOT RELATED TO WATER

Termites

Subterranean and Formosan termites are more problematic because they live in the soils on which the house is built. These termites do not need wet wood—they can infest your house when the wood frame is dry. These WDOs can build mud tubes from the soils into the wood frame of the building and then they live off the cellulose of the wood in the house. The result is that every day you have termites in your house, you have less house. Treatment can be more expensive and complicated as often the soils need to be treated and repeated treatments may be needed. Again, this means a complex repair to a core system, and that means the costs to repair are uncertain. Smart research will include understanding if termites are a problem in your area.

Rodents

Rodents, while not a WDO, are a common problem in homes in many parts of the country. Rodents can include rats, mice, squirrels, raccoons, and even river otters—you will not believe the mess river otters can make.

In some regions rodents can carry the hantavirus and other diseases, and even if they don't, they can make a mess and also raise concerns about indoor air quality. No one really wants rodents living in their house, even if it does not result in a quantifiable health risk. Have you ever heard the phrase, "I smell a rat"? Well, there is a good reason for that saying. Houses infested with rodents can have a horrible odor.

Some building configurations are especially prone to rodents. Houses that lack cohesive perimeter foundations—such as houses on post and pier foundations—are especially prone. Old houses are generally more prone to rodent problems than newer homes. This is because newer homes are built more tightly and generally have fewer possible openings into which rodents can enter the house.

Most rodent problems are discovered in the attic above the house, in the crawl space below the house, or in basements and garages; these are the places to check for rodents. Another good place to check is below the kitchen sink and under the dishwasher.

Generally, beware of houses with lots of trees touching the roof or vegetation around the house: This provides cover for rodents and tree limbs can act as a highway for rodents to get onto the roof and then into the attic. Try keeping trees pruned at least 6 feet from the house.

Red flags around the house include overgrown vegetation and chew marks on wood, such as in the eaves or around crawl space vents. Check for signs of prior rodent problems such as bait stations (pictured left), mousetraps, or rodent droppings (pictured right).

Rodents love fiberglass insulation. This is a perfect rodent-nesting material. Some houses simply do not lend themselves well to being insulated for this reason. Think, for example, of an old post and pier cabin—this was never designed to have subfloor insulation. When you go to insulate it, you change how the building will perform and you will most likely have created a rodent condominium since you

Rodent contamination on fiberglass insulation.

have installed nesting material without an adequate exclusion perimeter.

Tip: If you do wish to insulate an attic or subfloor, be sure and set some rodent traps first to see if the area can be successfully made rodent-proof.

Tip: If you want to insulate a space and you think it may be difficult or impossible to rodent-proof, such as a house with a post and pier foundation, consider using rigid or spray foam insulation. Rodents can still chew this insulation, but they may not want to nest in it. If you do use spray foam, make sure you hire an experienced and reputable contractor—this is a complex product and must be installed properly.

CONCLUSION

This chapter has given you a basic understanding about the importance of wood-destroying-organism inspections and you are now armed with some good tips or red flags to watch out for when touring houses.

THE BONES OF COMFORT 15

An older gentleman purchased a newly built home and was complaining to the builder that he was cold, especially when he read his newspaper in the kitchen nook—it had vaulted ceilings and big windows looking out to his yard. The builder came out, looked around, determined that the heat ducts were connected, and said, "It's not cold in here, you're just old!"

As you might imagine, this did not sit well with the new homeowner and for good reason. The new homeowner hired a colleague of mine who does infrared camera inspections. An infrared camera scan of his walls and ceilings revealed that the builder had forgotten to insulate the ceiling.

The moral of this story is that it is very hard to know for sure if a home is going to be comfortable without doing some time-consuming and expensive diagnostics. Even a newly constructed house can appear to be built well, but may not be comfortable or even as efficient as you imagined. More important, you may not really know if it is a comfortable or efficient home until you live in the house for a full year.

Given this uncertainty, it is important to understand how building construction and engineering have changed over the years. This will help you get a general idea of the relationship between comfort, efficiency, and durability in the home's construction and hopefully better align your expectations for home comfort. This background knowledge is very helpful when finding a house that truly "feels" like it fits.

THE HISTORY OF COMFORT

What are the clues to comfort? The first approach is to know your history. For example, if you are in the market for an old home, let's say one built around 1910, think back to what the world was like when your home was built. Model T Fords were just rolling off the assembly line, as was the Titanic, and less than a generation before, use of energy had switched from coal and whale oil to petroleum.

You can glimpse into this world by watching old silent films. If you look closely, you'll notice an amazing thing. Look for a scene that takes place in the winter: Do you notice that people sitting inside their homes are wearing wool sweaters and coats? It reminds me of a film in the 1970s where the lead character stands inside an elevator smoking a cigarette; people just don't do that anymore.

We have come to expect a lot more comfort from our homes than we used to. Kids today are accustomed to gallivanting about a house in shorts and tee shirts all winter. Can you imagine dining at a friend's house in the winter wearing a heavy sweater or wool coat today? You'd swelter!

Let's dig a little deeper to understand how comfort has changed over the last 150 years, and then we'll see how those changes affect the overall performance of a house.

DEFINE YOUR THERMAL ENVELOPE

The basic concept to keep a home comfortable, whether heating or cooling, is creating a thermal envelope between the inside of your house and the outside world. Think of your home as a simple insulated box with a thermostat that can control the "indoor" temperature.

Older homes did not have well defined thermal envelopes, or even any thermal envelopes, depending on when and where they were built. It is typical for walls and ceilings to have no insulation and many areas of the home are simply too connected to the outside world. Take, for example, the old attached garage: It has an uninsulated overhead door so the space is cold in the winter. Without cohesive thermal and air barriers in the walls and ceilings of your garage, you basically have a hole in your insulated box that goes through that big overhead door and then into your house. This creates discomfort in the floors above and walls adjacent to the garage, which leads to higher heating and cooling costs.

HOME PERFORMANCE WITH
ENERGY STAR

BEFORE

AFTER

Typical Home Improvements:

Ⓐ Sealing Air Leaks and Adding Insulation

Ⓑ Improving Heating and Cooling Systems

Ⓒ Sealing Ductwork

Ⓓ Replacing Windows

Ⓔ Upgrading Lighting, Appliances, and Water Heating Equipment

Ⓕ Installing Renewable Energy Systems

MYTH BUSTER: HEAT DOES NOT RISE

Despite what you may have learned in elementary school, heat does not rise.

It's surprising how few people actually know this. Many of my clients react with wide-eyed exclamations and incredulous protests when confronted with this fact.

Let me explain. It is true that hot air rises because it is lighter than cold air, just as hot water rises because it is lighter than cold water. But heat goes from concentrations of more to concentrations of less. Thus, if you have an uninsulated cold wall in your house, it will make your house cold. When you heat your home to make it comfortable, that cold wall will literally suck the heat right out of your house. If you don't believe me, try this: Stand next to an ice-cold wall and you will actually feel it pulling the heat from you too.

It is simple to make a home comfortable: Build a well insulated box that does not allow heat loss. Think of a portable thermos that keeps your coffee warm. Simple, right? Not quite.

AIR LEAKAGE

The truth is you need more than just a super-insulated box to keep a comfortable temperature that is warm or cool; you also will need an air-tight box. Unfortunately, older homes were not built with air leakage in mind. Did you know that many older homes have an equivalent air leakage similar to leaving the front door of the house wide open? No wonder older homes often have higher energy bills.

Older buildings lose heat in many places: chimneys, walls, ceilings, and floors. All buildings are also subject to something called the stack effect. Cold air infiltrates down low in the building and hot air escapes out the top of the building—just like a chimney. The stack effect is present in all buildings, but the more leaks in the house, the stronger the stack effect will be.

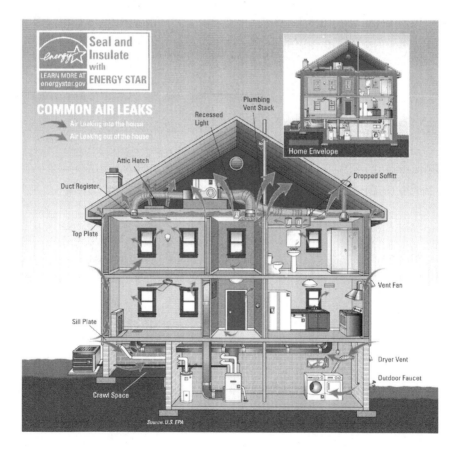

But this is also fixable, right? We just need to build a super-insulated and airtight box to separate the inside from the outside, and then we will have a comfortable home with low energy bills. Simple.

LIFE IS NEVER SIMPLE

As the old adage goes, "nothing simple is ever easy."

These balloons were pulled toward the fireplace due to the stack effect from the chimney sucking the air out of the house and up the flue.

Now imagine you have built yourself this perfect house. You are happily breathing, cooking, and cleaning; you can take a shower and the washing machine is working away. It is winter and you look out the window and notice that water is dripping down on the windowpane. All that moisture from your breathing and showering and cooking is now trapped inside your perfectly airtight, super-insulated box. There is a very good chance you have just constructed the perfect box to create mold and water problems!

Believe it or not, in the throes of the early 1970s energy crisis, which prompted the movement to better insulate our homes, many established builders insisted that all this insulation and air sealing was a terrible idea. They feared we would be creating sweatboxes. And they were right. Building a well insulated and airtight home comes with two inherent problems. The first problem is the home will trap moisture. The second problem is air no longer moves through the structure. We call air moving through a wall assembly "dry potential," and it was an important characteristic of our older homes that made them

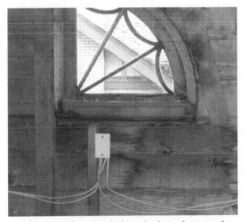

This window has clearly been leaking for years but the wood is very sound. Wood that gets wet does not rot. Wood that stays wet rots. This wall assembly had great dry potential in this old attic, especially with this decay-resistant old growth lumber.

Overall, it would be fair to say that while modern homes are likely to be more comfortable and energy efficient than older homes, they are also more susceptible to water damage than older buildings.

generally more durable and less susceptible to decay than our newer buildings. Also, our older building were constructed from old growth lumber, which is more resistant to decay than modern framing lumber and significantly more resistant to decay than modern engineered products like oriented strand board (OSB).

THE PASSIVE HOUSE

To understand how we can build well insulated and airtight homes today, it helps to look at an extreme example.

In Germany, they have created a type of house called the "passive house." These houses are so tight and so well insulated that even when they are located in a climate similar to Colorado, they do not need heat sources. Imagine a home with no heat bills!

These homes demonstrate the fact that heat does not rise; heat goes from hot to cold. With a perfectly airtight and super-insulated home, you don't need to keep generating new heat for your house: You can use heat coming off of lights and appliances and the rays of the sun to heat your house.

In a passive home, they substitute a standard heat source for something called a heat recovery ventilator. These systems are essentially a fan that takes outside air and moves it inside, and takes inside air and moves it outside. As this fan moves the air, it expels moisture and other pollutants from inside the building. At the same time, it limits heat loss by running the outgoing air through a heat exchanger so the outgoing air gives up its heat to the incoming air. In theory, this allows for unlimited ventilation with limited heat loss.

USE YOUR FANS

Most modern homes in the United States do not employ heat recovery ventilators so you are unlikely to see one. But most modern homes likely have a fan system, and that can be a critical part of keeping your home dry and preventing mold.

Unfortunately, the national building code has let us down when it comes to defining and regulating fresh air systems inside modern homes.

This is because there is not a single standard for creating air changes, nor control requirements for regulating indoor relative humidity. As a result, the typical homeowner knows little to nothing about air changes and indoor relative humidity. The consequences can be dire and can lead to dangerous indoor air quality and mold problems. (See image on page 118.)

TEMPERING HUMIDITY

Controlling indoor relative humidity is vital to reducing the risks from condensation such as the sweating you get on the inside of windows in the wintertime. There are essentially two times of year that can require different strategies for controlling indoor relative humidity.

Wintertime: Your goal should be trying to keep indoor relative humidity between 40 and 55 percent in the wintertime or when there are cold outdoor temperatures. Simply using bath and kitchen fans is often adequate. In the winter, running a fan will bring in cold dry air from outside, thus using fans helps to lower indoor relative humidity by replacing hot, wet interior air with cold, dry exterior air. This may seem counterintuitive when it is cold and rainy outside but even when it is pouring rain outside in the winter, that cold air does not hold much moisture. So when you bring it in and heat it to 70 degrees Fahrenheit, it will be relatively dry.

Summertime: The summertime goal for relative humidity is 60 percent or less. Controlling indoor relative humidity in the summer is more difficult because outdoor humidity rises and you can't replace interior wet air with outside dry air. Unless you have a central cooling system or use a dehumidifier, expect summer humidity to track roughly with the outdoor humidity. This can create serious condensation problems in hot humid climates when the hot summer air meets a cool air-conditioned wall. This is why people who live in places where it is humid in the summer use dehumidifiers in their basements.

Tip: You can buy a simple temperature and relative humidity

gauge at most hardware stores to help you monitor indoor relative humidity.

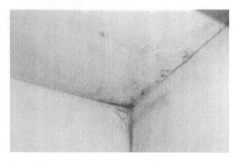

Tip: Look around windows, in bathrooms, on exterior walls, in closets, and on the sheathing of the attic for signs of mold that could indicate prior condensation issues. Note that if you are looking at a house in the summer, these clues may help you understand what it will be like in the house during the winter. It also may indicate that you'll need to improve the fresh air ventilation system in the house.

THERMOSTATS—THE KEYS TO THE KINGDOM OF COMFORT

Previously I mentioned my affinity for beach cabins, as I lived in a great one. It was a small 1940s cabin that was added onto in the 1960s. I lived there with my wife, a satellite colony of carpenter ants and several families of mice—we all loved it. Despite the fact that my wife was the only other member of the household sharing the rent, it was a beautiful property and a great fit for the lifestyle of young newlyweds.

But the heating system drove me crazy. The old cabin had electric baseboard heaters with no thermostats: Just those plastic knobs on the baseboards. If I turned that little knob a tiny bit too far to the right, I would wake as if I'd been placed in a roaring sauna. Turning the knob ever so slightly to the left and the next night I would be convinced the power had gone out and the pipes were on the verge of freezing.

Even though I lived in a poorly insulated cabin with an expensive-to-operate, lousy heating system, I could have been comfortable. All I needed was a $15 thermostat and this same building and heating system would have worked to keep the ants, the mice, and us perfectly comfortable.

The lesson: An accurate thermostat can be the key to comfort even in a crappy, poorly insulated house with a cheap, bare-bones heating system.

Thermostat Tip 1: When looking at and touring homes, see if the home has a thermostat. Some homes have multiple thermostats. We call this a "zoned" house because you can turn down the heat in one section of the house and turn it up in another section. This allows you to focus heat on the parts of the house where you want to be comfortable. If the house has no thermostats at all, expect an experience like we had in our cabin.

Thermostat Tip 2: One of the best paybacks for energy savings is to upgrade from a simple dial thermostat to a programmable thermostat. This can allow you to set back the temperature at night and during the day to save energy. Of course, this also means you need to take the time to actually *program* the thermostat.

FUEL CHOICES FOR HEAT

Generally, you have six choices of fuels to heat your home and keep it comfortable.

1. Natural Gas
2. Electricity — resistance heat and heat pumps
3. Propane
4. Oil
5. Wood/pellets
6. Passive solar

Energy prices fluctuate seasonally, regionally, nationally, and over time, so trying to understand the best fuel choice to heat you house can be complex.

5 GUIDING PRINCIPLES

1. Electricity and natural gas tend to be the most regulated, and the least likely fuel choices to have dramatic in-season changes. Oil and propane are more prone to seasonal price fluctuations.
2. Natural gas, if it is available, tends to give you the least expensive cost per BTU, as far as conventional heat sources go, when you factor in both the cost of the BTUs and the cost of the heating equipment. That's why the most common central heating sources are natural gas boilers and forced air furnaces.
3. Pellet stoves and wood stoves can have an even cheaper cost per BTU than natural gas but they are not as convenient or typical for central heating systems. They are especially cheaper when factoring in the cost of the equipment. These are usually not central heating systems.

4. Heat pumps are one of the least expensive costs per BTU and they have the benefit of being safe and providing cooling. Unfortunately, heat pumps are expensive to buy compared to other heating systems like a gas forced air furnace, so your up-front costs to install the equipment are higher.

5. If you were to generalize energy costs, the cost of a BTU in ascending order starting with the least expensive would be: solar, wood, wood pellets, heat pump, natural gas, propane, oil, electricity.[1]

Note: A BTU is a British Thermal Unit. A BTU is the amount of heat needed to raise the temperature of one pound of water by one degree Fahrenheit. It is also, apparently, a similar amount of heat as completely burning a four-inch wooden kitchen match.

Tip: If you are designing a heating and cooling system for your house, you may want to contact a local heating contractor. They often can break down the relative cost per BTU of different heating and cooling equipment and fuel choices in your area. They can also help you size your heating and cooling system appropriately by doing a heat loss calculation on your house. By investing a few dollars for this information, it may help you save hundreds or even thousands of dollars over time.

---

1. Please note this is just a rule of thumb that can change by season, date, region, and relative efficiency of the heating appliance. Also, this does not include the cost of the equipment, just the cost of the BTU.

HOUSE SAFETY, BUILDING CODES, AND LIABILITY **16**

More than just a promotional slogan, "A safe home is a happy home" is the essence of what every homeowner wants.

National building codes, which get adopted in different ways and in different magnitudes by cities and municipalities, are designed primarily as safety standards. They have been developed over the years as an effort to protect the public from unsafe building practices.

Interestingly, building codes are surprisingly unspecific about some important safety issues, such as requirements for an exterior envelope installation to protect against water intrusion as well as specific requirements for indoor air quality issues, such as mold. On the other hand, the building code is very specific—and even prescriptive—about other safety issues, such as how and where to install safety glass, how to build a safe stair system, and how to frame a house so that it can withstand regionally specific wind loads and earthquakes.

Some common safety issues are not well defined in the building code because some problems have no accurate means of measurement. The mold industry, for example, is a multi-billion dollar business that has few, if any, undebatable metrics. How much mold is too much? What species of mold are most harmful? Should you test for mold before you buy a house? Is mold on the roof decking, or inside an attic space, an indoor air quality issue? If you answer yes to this last question, what is your evidence to prove or disprove this?

Remember the principle that it's what you don't know that will hurt you. Unfortunately, there are some safety issues that can be difficult or even impossible to quantify. This is why people get so afraid about indoor air quality issues such as mold: It is easy to be afraid of what you cannot accurately measure or quantify.

When it comes to thinking of a home's safety, I like to break things down into three categories:

1. Building code safety
2. Indoor air quality
3. Environmental liability issues

The first is fairly prescriptive and the latter two are much more subjective and require some personal interpretation, judgment, and even testing.

Keep in mind that the topic of house safety is limitless and cannot be summarized in a book chapter. The discussions here are limited and oriented around the goal of better equipping you for looking at and comparing and contrasting houses. You are likely to run into other contractors, inspectors, or other professional who have varying opinions about some of these things. That is just how it is.

BUILDING CODES AND SAFETY

The first thing you need to understand about building codes is that they are primarily political documents. The procedures for changing and adopting building codes are Byzantine and like most political processes they are only vaguely influenced by reason, logic, and metrics.

This is not to diminish the importance and value of building codes. Look no further than the earthquakes that struck Haiti and then Chile in 2010. Chile is a relatively wealthy country with a history of strong building codes that date back to a 9.5 magnitude earthquake in 1960 that was the largest earthquake ever measured. The massive 8.8 quake of 2010 caused a tsunami and extensive damage, yet only 500 people died and most of those deaths were associated with the tsunami. In Haiti, by contrast, a much smaller 7.0 magnitude earthquake nearly destroyed the country. The death toll from this smaller quake is staggering. Accurate counts are not even available, but the most conservative estimates exceed 100,000 deaths. It is undeniable that building codes have the potential to save lives.

The next thing to understand about building codes is that they are not guarantees of perfect house construction. Many quality builders and home inspectors think of building codes as bare minimum standards; it is essentially illegal to build a house to a lesser standard. Quality construction will often exceed these standards.

When it comes to safety items that are prescribed in the building code, a lot depends on the city building officials who oversaw the construction of the home. Remember, once the walls go up, there is a lot that a home inspector can no longer see. This is why home inspectors use clues about what they can see to tell them if they should be worried about what they cannot see.

It is important to understand that home inspectors do *not* perform code-compliant inspections. It is not feasible to cohesively apply modern building standards to older buildings. It should be understood that what we consider "safe" changes over time. Older buildings are generally considered "grandfathered," but there are systems and installations in older buildings that may be considered unsafe by today's standards. The extent to which a home inspector calls out modern standards for safety during a home inspection is subjective; it can be unclear whether a condition pointed out by an inspector is a repair item or an improvement item.

For example, if you are in an older house that has no ground fault protection (GFCI) for the bathroom sink outlets, this is a safety issue that should really be repaired; installation of a $15 electric receptacle with a reset button could save your life. But, isn't this also an improvement item if GFCIs were not required for the bathroom receptacles when the house was built? What if the bathroom was recently remodeled? This is an example of the kind of gray area that home inspectors are constantly muddling into.

GUIDING PRINCIPLES OF BUILDING SAFETY CODES

1. Older houses in rural areas tend to have less oversight of construction from building officials than newer homes built in more established and densely populated towns. In other words, you are more likely to find construction without permits or that no building official ever inspected.
2. Older homes had less stringent safety standards than modern homes so they are generally less safe.

You don't need to know building code to be an educated home-buyer. If you are interested, there are a plethora of resources that can teach you about building codes and building safety, though a thorough understanding of building codes and safety can take years of study and practice. Below, we will discuss a few items that are most relevant to helping you look at and compare homes.

STAIRS

An astonishing number of accidents occur on stairs: According to the National Safety Council, over 1 million injuries each year and an estimated 12,000 deaths annually can be attributed to falls on stairs.

One study estimated that every year nearly 100,000 children are injured or hospitalized from falls on stairs; when averaged over a year, this translates into one hurt child every six minutes. This should explain why many home inspectors spend a tremendous amount of time fussing over seemingly silly stair details in a home.

Old Homes and Stairs

If I am inspecting a 100-year-old home and I find that all of the stairs meet modern safety standards, you could knock me over with a feather. It almost never happens, so you need to have some perspective.

Some old homes have second floors and basements with exceptionally marginal and unsafe stairs. This makes these spaces less usable and less valuable. Think about the impact on resale: People not interested in buying your house could include older couples, handicapped people, and families with young children—anyone who might feel they cannot safely navigate the stairs.

Other old stair systems are just slightly unsafe; these are often just a code cycle or two away from modern standards. These are more common and fortunately, not usually a significant safety hazard.

For the purposes of looking at homes, you should ask yourself how critical stair systems are to you and be cognizant of spaces accessed by steep or unsafe stairs.

DECKS

Decks are so often built without a permit that I am sometimes shocked when I see a code-built decking system. Collapsing decks cause hundreds of injuries annually in the United States and some deck collapses result in fatality. Be sure your home inspector checks the construction of any decks on houses you are proposing to buy. When touring homes, you can often spot old or shoddy deck construction without being an expert. Just look carefully and critically:

- Do you see bolts holding the ledger board to the house?
- Is the guardrail stiff or loose?
- Do you see rotted or damaged decking boards?
- When you jump up and down on the deck, does it feel stiff or does it feel like it might fall over?

WINDOWS AND EGRESS

This deck was not properly attached to the building and could collapse under weight.

Unless the windows in an older home have been cohesively updated, expect that older houses will have at least some safety issues regarding windows. Window safety issues come in four basic forms:

1. Safety glass such as tempered or laminated glass
2. Egress (the ability to get safely in and out of windows)
3. Falling hazard for children
4. Sash weights

Safety Glass

Safety glass comes in two types: tempered and laminated. Think of these as similar to the glass on the windshield of a car—if it breaks, it spider webs and does not fall apart into sharp shards that could cut or kill. Both tempered and laminated glass will have small etched logos on the glass for proper identification. Code requirements for safety glass are complicated enough that I have spent all day at seminars learning about their proclivities. Safety glass will not impact your house hunting but a good home inspector may point out some places where we would use safety glass in a modern house so you are aware of these potential safety concerns.

Fire Egress

Fire egress is another example of a code that has changed over the years. Egress just means that windows should be located so that a fireman can come into the house to save your life. All bedrooms should have a legal fire egress. For legal fire egress, a window should be no more than 44 inches off the floor and should have at least a 5.7-square-foot opening. If you see bedrooms with windows that look difficult to get out of, you should question whether this is really a bedroom or just staged that way. I see staged bedrooms all the time that are unsafe because they do not have safe fire egress, especially in remodeled basements. This is a serious safety concern that you should look for during home touring. Cutting in a proper sized window is often quite easy but it can cost between $1,000 and $3,000, so absence of a safe egress window in a bedroom is a real safety and monetary concern.

This is not a legal bedroom and has inadequate window egress.

Falling Hazard for Children

Because fire egress codes want to allow a safe way for firemen to get into your home, the same safe and code-compliant window can actually pose a safety hazard for small children. If you have children on the second floor of a house with low windows that they could crawl out of, consider looking for a window barricade. These are designed to keep your child safely inside the house, but they can also be disabled by firemen in an emergency. These are not required by code but may be an improvement you want to look into.

Sash Weights

These are the counter-weights used in old wood windows where you see a rope attached to the lower window sash. When these ropes break, there is no longer a counter balance to the weight of this sash. If you open a window with missing sash weights and let go, the window will come crashing down and can even shatter the glass. Now imagine that your child's hand or even head was in the way. These are called guillotine windows. Missing ropes on sash weights should always be repaired or the window should be securely locked closed.

Note the broken/missing sash rope on this old window.

INDOOR AIR QUALITY

Lead and Asbestos

If you are buying a home built prior to 1978, there is a good chance that at least some building materials in the home will contain lead and/or asbestos. If your plans are to just move into an older home and live your life, you are unlikely to be exposed to these substances in a significant way. This is because the toxic substances in question are encapsulated below layers of paint and inside of finishes. Encapsulated toxic materials are difficult to aerosolize, which means the substances are unlikely to become airborne particulates that you could breathe. Remember: *There are millions of people safely living in older homes that have lead and asbestos.*

If, however, you have remodeling plans that include tearing down walls, or removing or sanding old wood trim, then the risk of exposure is very real and you should plan accordingly.

Your best bet if you are tearing into any part of an older house, creating any kind of dust from refinishing, or altering the building materials in an old house, you should work closely with a qualified general contractor who is trained in remediation techniques for lead and asbestos.

Laws regarding asbestos could vary by state but many states will require

- Homeowners to test for asbestos prior to any construction or renovation project
- Contractors to obtain a written asbestos report from a building owner prior to work
- Asbestos remediation to be done by licensed abatement contractors prior to starting demolition work

Please note that most home inspectors will *not* test for these materials. Other home inspectors will but they will charge an additional "testing fee" because of the work involved. You may also choose to hire a specialist, such as an environmental lab, that will perform detailed testing for you. In my experience, most homebuyers do not do this testing as part of their due diligence when buying a house.

The bottom line is you need to decide how much risk you are willing to take. Most people are comfortable buying older homes—we all grew up in them! But if you cannot sleep at night because you are so worried about the dangers of lead and asbestos, consider purchasing a home newer than 1978.

Overall, you should

- Expect there to be lead and asbestos containing materials in any house older than 1978.
- Plan on doing detailed testing and remediation before you do any remodel work to the house that would create significant dust and air-borne particulate.
- Have detailed testing done by a specialist if you feel you need to know this information prior to purchase.

- Consider the dangerous realities of exposing your family to these toxic substances if you plan on renovating an older house while living in it.

Common Places to Find Asbestos-Contaminated Materials:

- Boiler pipe insulation and old boiler equipment
- Old heating equipment and old white tape wrapping ductwork (pictured below)

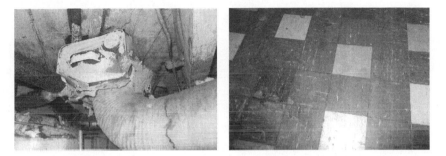

- Old 9 × 9 floor tiles (pictured above)
- Popcorn ceilings installed prior to 1978
- Vermiculite insulation (an insulating material made from a mineral that has been mined from the earth)

WHAT ABOUT MOLD?

A moisture problem inside a home often has a homebuyer asking, "Is this creating mold?" and "Will this be harmful to my health?"

While those are excellent questions, even doctors struggle to quantify health risks associated with mold-related indoor air quality problems. True data is especially elusive given the myriad variables that include the people involved, the length of the exposure, and the species of mold.

Here is what you need to know:

Prolonged exposure to high levels of *any* species of mold can be harmful to human health. Even if you are not "allergic" to mold now, you could develop a mold allergy given prolonged exposure. Armed with this, what should you know about mold to be prepared to think about houses and compare and contrast them?

The most important thing to understand is that we have only *one* way to control or eliminate mold in our buildings—stopping the water. By ensuring that our homes are dry, we virtually eliminate chances for mold growth and exposure. Thus the presence of mold in a house is a symptom. Mold is not the problem; water is the problem.

Looking for the Source of Mold

When it comes to mold, think of breaking moisture problems into two categories: chronic and localized.

Localized water problems could easily result in mold growth. Think about the sheetrock below a leaky pipe fitting. While this leak will create mold on the sheetrock, the real problem is the plumbing leak. Once the leak is repaired, the mold-covered materials could be sealed or removed, and your problem gone. Also, keep in mind that small areas of localized mold are not likely to cause significant health problems, as your exposure is limited. Professionals often consider localized mold problems to be anything less than a 4 × 8 foot piece of building material.

Chronic water problems inside a building can easily result in poor indoor air quality and a safety hazard for the  occupants. You should be looking for signs of chronic moisture conditions inside any home you look at and your home inspector should alert you to any signs of chronic water problems uncovered during a home inspection. Chronic water problems can result in a slew of bad things for your house, including damage to finishes, the structure, and unsafe indoor air quality. Homes with chronic moisture problems are not homes with good bones.

Chronic moisture problems in buildings can be expensive to correct and typically result from some combination of four primary moisture sources.

1. Leaking/failing roofs and exterior envelopes
2. Chronic drainage problems
3. Chronic plumbing problems
4. Chronic high indoor humidity

Chronic failure in roof, exterior, plumbing, and drainage systems tend to be straight-forward for home inspectors to find and identify; even an inexperienced layperson can often identify a badly failing roof or water damage from extensive plumbing problems. It is harder to detect latent and concealed defects, and even trickier when there are chronic high relative humidity problems.

Despite what you may see on TV, home inspectors are not allowed to do destructive testing as part of the typical home buying process. Home inspections are visual, and when it comes to mold issues, this limits the ability of an inspector to find latent moisture problems lurking behind walls or in ceiling cavities.

Home inspectors are accustomed to working with this limitation. Experienced home inspectors are good at seeking clues and red flags that could indicate hidden moisture or mold problems. When such clues are discovered, your home inspector should direct you to seek a specialist to further investigate a potential problem.

Mold Specialists and Testing

Mold specialists come in two basic forms: testing and remediation. Some specialists can do both types of testing.

While mold testing seems like a great idea, the information gleaned from testing has serious limitations. Building Science Corporation, a consulting architecture firm that specializes in building technology consulting, offers a terrific online guide worth reading.[1]

This brief guide will help you gain a nuanced understanding regarding the limitations of mold testing. In short, many indoor air quality experts share the opinion that *limited resources are best spent diagnosing and fixing moisture problems* rather than spending precious resources on mold testing. If prolonged exposure to high levels of *any* species of mold can be harmful to human health, does it matter what species you are dealing with? Or should you simply address the underlying moisture problem? This point of view may change regionally; I know that some regions of the country have problems with some particular toxic strains of mold, in which case a more conservative testing protocol may be warranted.

Mold remediation specialists can help you diagnose and repair building moisture problems. These companies can diagnose the various ways a building can get wet, including building science problems of high relative humidity and condensing surfaces. They should help you identify and stop water problems and then seal or remove contaminated materials.

---

1. See http://www.buildingscience.com/documents/reports/rr-0209-mold-testing.

Don't expect your home inspector to be able to quantify the potential health risks from a given mold condition; do expect a good home inspector to alert you to red flags that could indicate water problems in a perspective home that could in turn lead to indoor air quality problems.

Common Mold Myths

Here's something nearly every home inspector will hear at some point from a client: "That's black mold!" said in a horrified voice. In reality, this is like screaming "green trees!" Just because mold is black does not necessarily make it any more or less likely to harm you, despite what you may have seen on TV. Instead of freaking out, if you see mold, remember you are looking at a moisture problem. The solution is to diagnose and fix the water problem and then remove or seal whatever the substance is. Lots of mold equals a large and complex moisture problem. Localized mold means a localized and manageable water problem.

RADON

Radon is a radioactive gas that comes from natural uranium deposits in the soils, rock, and water around your house. Many parts of the country are known to have homes with high radon levels that cause unsafe indoor air quality.

If you are buying a home in an area with this risk, you should have the home tested for radon during your contingency period. Ask your real estate professional and your home inspector if testing for radon is a common practice in your area and plan accordingly.

Each year many thousands of lung cancer deaths can be attributed to radon gas exposure. This is an issue that should be taken seriously. Radon gas exposure is responsible for more lung cancer deaths than any other cause, second only to smoking cigarettes. The good news is that cost-effective radon prevention systems work and can limit radon exposure.

LIABILITY: OIL TANKS, SEWER LINES, AND SEPTIC SYSTEMS

Oil Tanks

On a scale of good to bad, buying a house with an abandoned and leaking oil tank falls distinctly onto the bad side of the ledger. The good news is that properties with these tanks are rare, but they do exist and oil cleanup can be expensive—the insurance for oil spills in my state covers up to $60,000 in cleanup costs! Here's how to spot a home that might have a buried oil tank and a few tips on how to protect yourself from costly cleanup fees if oil from the tank were to leak or if oil contamination is found on your property.

Typical above ground oil tank.

Homes with Active Oil Heat

If you are a homeowner and you have active oil heat (meaning your current heating system runs on oil), you should look into getting it covered by insurance. In Washington State, as an example, you can register your tank through the Pollution Liability Insurance Agency (PLIA), which offers free insurance to anyone in the state who registers with the program. If you are buying a property with active oil heat, make sure that the current owner has registered the tank. If they have not, you should register the tank as soon as you take ownership of the property.

As a general rule, the longer the history of coverage, the better; this allows less opportunity for the insurance program to claim a pre-existing condition if a claim is filed. I would research to see if your state has a similar insurance program.

Homes with Inactive Oil Heat

Gas meter.

The last four decades have seen a dramatic shift away from oil and toward natural gas as the fuel used to heat houses. The reason for this shift is two-fold: oil is more expensive than natural gas and oil prices are volatile and subject to spikes.

Keep in mind that natural gas is a relatively new product.

In the Seattle area, natural gas started to be piped to our homes in the late 1950s. Therefore, most homes that were built prior to the late 1950s likely had oil heat at one time, even if they now have natural gas.

You could put these older natural-gas-powered homes into two categories:

1. Old houses with properly decommissioned or removed oil tanks
2. Old houses with abandoned oil tanks

In my experience, most oil tanks have been properly decommissioned. This is when a professional contractor empties the tank and either cleans and fills the tank or removes it. However, beware of the property with active natural gas heat and an abandoned oil tank. Such a property may not be covered under an insurance program if the heating system were fueled by natural gas. If oil contamination were found on that site, the owner of the property could be responsible to clean it up. Remember that $60,000 insurance?

How to Find a Buried Oil Tank That May Have Been Abandoned

On the outside, look for the presence of a gas meter *and* an oil tank fill valve (pictured bottom) and/or a breather tube (pictured top). If the oil tank has been properly decommissioned, they will usually remove or cut the breather tube and fill valve so there will be no signs of an oil tank on the outside of the house. Presence of *both* a gas meter and an oil tank outside the house indicate that there may be an abandoned tank.

On the inside of the house, go to where the furnace is installed and look for small copper lines (pictured

Top: Oil tank breather tube—easy to locate. Bottom: Oil tank fill valve—usually located outside. These are often difficult to find because they frequently get buried or obstructed by vegetation if the tank has been abandoned.

right). They often come as a set and the copper tubes will usually be pinched on the ends. This tells you the house was once heated using oil and may have a buried oil tank.

What to Do if You Suspect You Have a Buried Oil Tank

If you are concerned the property has an abandoned and buried oil tank that might be leaking (or might leak in the future), you'll want to have the property evaluated by a contractor who specializes in oil tank location and decommissioning. Try to have the tank decommissioned by

Copper oil lines—usually located in the basement.

the seller prior to your taking ownership of the property; that way if problems arise in the decommissioning, you are not the owner of the property when it happens.

If you do not see evidence of a buried oil tank outside but you find evidence inside, do not just assume the tank has been decommissioned. Ask the seller for a copy of a decommissioning statement. I would add this to the title of the property so if you lose the statement, there is a permanent record of the decommissioning. When you go to sell the house, you'll want to have this statement to pass along to the new owners.

Please note that these guidelines and principles will vary regionally. This information is limited in scope and does not cover some of the more complicated scenarios that can arise with oil tanks such as soil testing. Be sure to seek the advice of local experts in your area when buying a house.

SEWER SCOPES AND SEPTIC INSPECTIONS

One item of liability that is often not covered in a home inspection is sewer lines and septic systems. Sewer lines and septic systems are how you dispose of sewage from your house. Repairs to sewer lines and septic systems can be expensive and you don't generally get your money back on this type of repair work—it's not like remodeling your kitchen.

Sewer Lines

In the case of sewer lines, these are pipes in the ground that connect your house to a city sewer system. If the pipes between your house and the city sewer have been damaged or no longer slope to drain, you could get nasty backups into the house and you could be responsible to repair these pipes.

A simple diagnostic you can do for sewer lines is to have the sewer scoped. This involves hiring a company to run a camera down the sewer line to check for cracks, breaks, and proper slope. They should also identify the type of pipe you have and how reliable the pipes should be in the future.

Septic Systems

When you get out into the country, the houses are too far apart to make it cost effective to run a city sewer, so most homes in rural locations have on-site septic systems. Septic systems are basically a holding tank that holds the solids and a series of drainpipes in the ground where the gray water runs. Septic systems are like little bacteriological factories in your yard that help to decompose waste. Every 4 to 5 years or so, you typically need to have your tank pumped out by a septic pump service. Some modern septic systems can get complex with UV filters and sand filters; some of these systems require annual or even biannual inspections and maintenance.

If you are buying a home with a septic system, you can often hire a third party who will inspect the septic system and tell you if it requires repair. You can usually learn more from your Realtor or the local health department regarding standard inspection procedures in your area. Many local counties will require a special health letter from the health department as part of a real estate transaction to ensure the septic is performing as intended.

CONCLUSION

This chapter has given you some basic tools for understanding how building codes work, some common safety issues in homes to be aware of, and some common liabilities found in buried oil tanks and sewer and septic systems. This may not impact how you look at a house, but these can be critical factors in moving forward with making an offer on a home.

Some homebuyers, knowing the risks with sewer lines, for example, decide to inspect the sewer before even doing the home inspection so that they know they can clear one hurdle before spending all their due diligence money at one time. In other cases, you may decide not to make an offer on a house simply because the unsafe stairs to the basement would be too great a risk in your life. These are the decisions you get to make as a homebuyer. When you look at houses with eyes wide open, these issues should not suddenly blindside you in the midst of a home inspection. You should be more prepared to face these challenges head-on and this knowledge may even save you an inspection fee as you may now recognize some safety or liability issues before you even get to schedule a home inspection.

CHEAT SHEET 17
COMMON PROBLEMS
AND HOUSE TRENDS

THE TOP 20

One of the advantages of looking at thousands of houses is coming to know where to expect problems. Below, I have included my top 20 guiding principles—maintenance and design trends that I see commonly in my region. Now that you have the background from reading chapters 1 through 16, I hope you find yourself prepared to understand and digest this cheat sheet; it should act as a simple review of materials.

Note: Inspectors in other areas could modify this list slightly with regional nuance, but I suspect these hold relatively true throughout the country.

LOCATIONS

1. **Exposed Lots:** Exposed lots with big views are more likely to have siding and envelope problems since big views equal exposure. The bigger the view, the more maintenance the exterior envelope will require.

2. **Steep Hillsides:** Look for signs of settlement in the structure or drainage problems, as water could be running toward the house. Look for erosion and sloughing soils around the property. Look for leaning trees, which could indicate unstable hillsides. You may want to hire a soils engineer or geotech to further investigate the property and give you a more detailed analysis of soil conditions.

3. **Low Lots:** Water is always trying to find the low spot. If you build a house in a low spot, the water is more likely to find it and persist.

4. **Rural Versus City:** The farther you get from a major city, the more random and inconsistent the house construction will get.

AGE

1. **Old Houses—Prior to 1940s:** Structure and site work problems are more common and wiring and plumbing and heating systems often need cohesive updates if it has not been done. Look for settlement and see what has been updated as far as disposable and entrenched systems.

2. **15-to-20-Year Rule:** Hitting the end of a maintenance life cycle. Expect the need for updating if it has not already been done: roof, deck, furnace, appliances, kitchens and bathrooms, flooring, and paint can all be on the table.

3. **1990s:** Look for recalled products (especially siding and water piping) and be aware of the 20-year life cycle problem and the fact that this was a transition decade—going from the way we used to build to the way we build today.

4. **1970s and Newer:** Newer homes are more likely to have better wiring and better structures and foundations than older homes. They are also more likely to have moisture problems. Higher probability of mold problems related to tightening of houses and resulting high relative humidity. Less decay-resistant building materials means more problems with exterior envelopes and wood decay.

DESIGNS AND INSTALLATIONS

1. **Atrium Skylights:** This is where there is a skylight and window all in one. These are commonly installed by kitchen sinks and in master bathrooms. Water can drain down the skylight onto the siding below the window, rotting the siding. Look for wood decay below these.

2. **Modern Wood Windows:** These are not made from old-growth wood. The wood is not as resistant to decay. Modern wood windows can be high maintenance, especially when exposed. Look

for rot on windows and expect high-maintenance painting costs if exposed to the weather.

3. **Stucco and Synthetic Stucco:** Stucco is a beautiful cladding system and when installed well, it can last the life of the building. Stucco does especially well in dry climates and on buildings with generous roof overhangs. However, stucco is very installation sensitive and can lead to expensive and difficult-to-see envelope problems. Be especially wary of 1990s era stucco and especially exposed stucco with wood windows. Be most wary of synthetic stucco siding systems; there have been many class-action lawsuits regarding this material.

4. **Wood Chimney Chases:** These wood boxes have metal chimney flues running inside and they stick up into the sky and collect water and rot. Expect to find wood decay in wood chimney chases that are over 20 years old or at least a need for regular caulking and painting.

5. **In-Swing Exterior Doors:** Exterior doors that are exposed to the weather are all vulnerable to leakage, but especially in-swing doors and especially French-style doors (where there are two swinging doors in one unit).

Note the water stains and swelling trim, indicating door leakage.

6. **Rooftop Decks:** There are two kinds of rooftop decks: the ones that leak and the ones that are going to leak. Be especially wary of rooftop decks done in ceramic or stone tile.

Water stains are a small clue that water is seeping around the rooftop deck/wall juncture.

259

7. **Windows Inside Shower Enclosures:** The easy way to fix this is simply build a shower curtain that covers your window. If left unchecked and shower water washes over the inside of the window for years, it's a near certainty that water will damage the window, the wall below the window or both.

8. **Lack of Roof Overhangs:** Buildings that lack roof overhangs are exposed to the weather and are more likely to have exterior envelope problems, especially if combined with flat roofs or rooftop decks.

9. **Wet Crawl Spaces:** Crawl spaces with drainage problems are likely to show other signs of high relative humidity problems. Look for molds on the roof decking, around windows, behind toilets, and in closets on exterior walls.

10. **Turrets, Curves, and Flat Roofs:** Simplicity is your friend and turrets and curving exterior walls do not represent simplicity—they are difficult to flash and hard to execute well. Be sure to look for water problems. Flat roofs are the same—if they do not shed water well, they are likely to be more vulnerable to leaks. In general, look to see if exterior details slope to drain.

11. **Buildings or Spaces that Started as One Thing and are Now Something Else:** The best example of this is an outbuilding that began as a garage and is now a heated yoga studio or apartment; or old basements that are now finished. Do you suppose that the concrete slabs were ever water proofed? Probably not. The building was not designed to have carpet and heat on the floor. This

change in purpose can often lead to some chronic problems in these spaces—especially moisture problems.

12. **Basements Get Wet:** Basements are a hole in the ground lined with concrete, which is essentially a large rigid sponge. Expect basements to get damp at least seasonally, and be sure your expectations for the basement space are appropriate. This gets truer the older the house is.

CONCLUSION

Your house is likely the most expensive thing you will ever buy in your life, but it is so much more than an asset. In the crude way that we calculate an asset, a house is an assemblage of tens of thousands of components installed somewhat haphazardly by hundreds of different people over an untold number of years or generations and influenced in a million unique ways by region, architecture, style, economy, building codes, climate, decorating trends, technology, and the whimsy of homeowners. Yet in another sense, a house is a sacred place; it is your temple, the place where many of your most precious daily rituals will transpire: bacon and eggs with your grandma, a ball game in the TV room with your sister, a snuggled up bedtime story, decorating the Christmas tree, lighting the fireplace on a cold winter evening, oiling the chain of your bike in the garage with your dad, taking in the sunset with your husband, scribing the growth of your child on the door jamb. These events shape our lives and the memories of these events survive in these homes you will be looking to call your own.

You need to go into homebuying aware of both the asset you are acquiring and the future that it will hold. You cannot and should not eliminate the emotion of buying a house and you cannot eliminate risk when buying houses. However, you can approach your purchase from a place of awareness and knowledge when it comes to the bones, design, and structural components of what you are buying.

There is a lot of hard-won house wisdom in this book. I have crawled through thousands of rodent-infested crawl spaces and been on thousands of roofs and looked at thousands of furnaces and electric panels and worked with thousands of prospective homebuyers and this is a boiled-down essence of what I have learned. I encourage you to go back and review sections to help these concepts sink in. You are learning a philosophy of how to look at and understand houses. The more you learn these techniques, the more buying a house will become a calculated and logical process and less of an emotional roller coaster. In the end, this knowledge will make you a better homebuyer and a better homeowner. You will be more likely to have your expectations in alignment with what you are buying, which is the key to happy home ownership. This awareness can save you countless headaches and thousands of dollars and can make the process of house hunting less scary and intimidating and more fun, exciting, and rewarding.

I hope this information helps you with your life as a homeowner. Best of luck on your house hunting!

Dylan Chalk
Orca Inspection Services, LLC

INDEX

ABOUT DYLAN CHALK

Dylan Chalk is the owner of Orca Inspection Services, LLC, a home inspection company serving the greater Seattle and North Kitsap region. His business goal has always been to assist his homebuying clients to see and understand the homes they are proposing to buy. Fulfillment of this goal has led to the publication of *The Confident House Hunter*, a book designed to help people become more aware of the houses they live in and the architecture and engineered environment that they interact with daily. It also spawned the founding of ScribeWare, LLC, a software company specializing in easy-to-use and easy-to-read inspection reports for a variety of construction-related fields.

A native New Englander and graduate of Colorado College, Dylan, his wife, and twin sons live on an island in Puget Sound. His favorite moments are those he spends with his family; together they enjoy skiing, hiking, biking, fishing, cooking, and music as well as working in their vegetable garden and pursuing the endless projects of home ownership.